"This is what the Lord says: 'Stand
at the crossroads
for the ancient
where the good way is, and
walk in it, and you will find
rest for your souls." (Jeremiah 6:16 NIV)

Enjoy!

Michael
Prichard

# BETTER THAN WELL

One Man's Miraculous Journey through
Childhood Trauma, Mental Illness,
Addiction, and Incarceration
to Joy and Contentment

## Michael Prichard M.S.

Covenant
Training and Consulting

ISBN: 978-1-66785-847-0 (printed)

ISBN: 978-1-66785-848-7 (eBook)

# BETTER THAN WELL

Disclaimer: This book is a memoir that reflects the author's recollection of experiences over time. Most people have been left unnamed and some events have been condensed to protect the privacy of certain individuals.

# CONTENTS

# FOREWORD

When Michael first contacted me to read his memoir, I was a little surprised. I had met him in church, and my daughter worked with him at the County, but we were acquaintances at best, and I only had a vague familiarity with his story.

As I read his words for the first time, I marveled at how God had transformed the man on the page into the man I now knew. I've read through these pages many times, each time going through a gamut of emotions. Anger and grief on behalf of a wounded child, fear of an out-of-control man, and finally awe at a loving God, who would go to any length to reach one of His own.

This is not just Michael's story. This is truly God's story. This is the story of God who leaves the 99 to find the one lost sheep. The God who desires none to perish but for all to come to repentance. God is between every line and inhabits each word.

And finally, I feel like I have truly met Michael. He is the man who God has raised up, using his experiences, his heartache, and his triumphs to be God's hands and feet; to speak the truth, and to love those who feel unlovable. He is the man who now stands in the gap for wounded, hurting people because he truly knows what it's like to be a wounded, hurting person.

Michael's story is unique but not unusual because God is in the habit of reaching out to those on the edge of society. He gives hope to the hopeless and He brings joy to those who sorrow.

No matter where you are in life, I happened to know you are loved by a very real and awesome God.

~ **Shawna Guzman**

# PREFACE

I first shared my story at a small church in Fresno, California shortly after I was paroled from prison in 2006. The emotional impact my story had on those in attendance surprised me then and every time I have shared it since. Numerous people in various contexts have suggested I write a book that would expand on the story I use when speaking in church settings.

Recovery stories are common, and I was not sure an expanded version of my story would have a greater impact than my shorter version. I also had difficulty understanding why anyone would be interested in reading a book written by a relatively unknown person. And, when I'm being honest, I didn't want to invest the emotional energy into writing something that might not help anyone.

After years of working in human service arenas, and much internal debate, I realized every story is unique and has the power to encourage others. Even mine. And perhaps I needed to tell the story of my recovery as much as someone else might need to hear it.

I typically do not share many details of my recovery when speaking in public venues. I usually talk about the factors that contributed to my problems, what it was like to live in the hell of addiction and mental illness and at the end say, "I am better today." Amazingly, people almost never inquire further, and those that have seemed to shut down when I mentioned God.

As a community educator on addiction and its associated problems, I try hard to organize and explain concepts so the audience can understand. But how do I explain how God helped me recover in a secular context? How do I convey a spiritual story about my experience with the God of the Bible to a group of people who don't have a unified understanding of who God is or may not even give credence to His existence, let alone those who may be hostile to the idea of God?

But in holding back the details, I have failed to tell my full story. My task is not to explain God but to tell my experience in the hope that people will see God in the story. Flawed as I am (and I am flawed in significant ways), perhaps my greatest contribution will be that I revealed something of God to others and, more important, reveal how He can reach into lives and transform them.

Despite continuous encouragement from others, I delayed writing my story for several reasons. For a long time, I did not feel that my restoration had reached a point where it was time to write. In other words, I was too busy rebuilding my life with God's oversight to write about my past.

Part of the recovery process involved the pursuit of life goals that would stabilize and establish me. I have come to the end of sixteen years of hard work, and I have accomplished the goals I set for myself. Everything I achieve now that goes beyond what I initially set out to do is simply extra. More, I have reached a place of contentment and stability through God's grace. Contentment in this world is a miracle in and of itself.

The second reason I delayed writing this book is that I did not want my pain and struggles and the pain I caused others to define my life and legacy. My time adrift in deep darkness traumatized me in ways I did not begin to comprehend until years into my recovery. Others who got close to me suffered as well. When I first got clean and sober, I imagined my old life as a pile of junk that I set on fire and walked away, letting it burn to ashes. I hated who I had become, and I'm not too fond of the remnants of that person that still linger. I didn't want to enter that darkness again to write about it.

Over the years, I have learned that it is impossible to separate my present from my past. My past informs my present. Not only are the past and present inseparable, but the achievement of life goals, by God's grace, shines the brightest against the dark backdrop that was my prior life. God's relationship to my existence and experiences are the only significant things about me. God shows me grace for reasons I cannot fully grasp.

The truth is, recovery from addiction and severe mental illness is not something I achieved in my own effort, rather, it is something that God did for me. I believe that God has a purpose for my suffering and that He has and will use that suffering for His glory, my good, and the good of others. So, for me, this meant that it was time to begin writing.

A few years ago, a colleague asked me if healing is something God did for me, and humans cannot replicate it for the benefit of others, what good is my story? I understand people are always searching for solutions to complex problems to produce consistent positive outcomes for the greatest number of people. As a former patient, I am convinced that there are categories of human pain that are beyond the reach of counselors, therapists, and physicians to remedy. I experienced some of those categories of pain. Healing from pains of these types is God's work (though He often uses people and systems to provide various levels of grace).

Many problems in this world are beyond human intervention (though we do not like to admit it), but none beyond God's ability, which is why miraculous stories of hope are so important. There are so many people drowning in the dark waters of despair, and often family and friends feel helpless to save them. For those people, hope is often all there is. This is especially true when all attempts at the best available treatments the world offers fail to yield any long-lasting results and even worsen conditions like in my case.

The purpose of this book is not to dissuade anyone from seeking clinical or medical help. After all, I am a certified substance use disorder counselor working in secular spaces. Secular treatment models, including the use of medication, can and often do help people achieve some stability in their lives. I have seen it firsthand and have experienced temporary relief myself. All available avenues of help should be pursued.

However, these may not be the ultimate solution when the pain and associated problems are rooted in existential angst and persistent hopelessness about life's purpose. When I counsel clients in the course of my work, I do not violate my professional code of ethics by imposing my worldview onto them, but this book contains my story. I will not be writing as Michael, the addiction professional. I am writing as Michael, the empty, hopeless, broken man made whole by the power of God.

This story is written primarily from my perspective and reflects how I experienced, internalized, processed, and interpreted the events that contributed to the problems I encountered at different stages of my life. As such, this book was in no way written with the intention of hurting or misrepresenting anyone and was not written to serve as a scholarly work. The reader should know that this book moves slow for the first 9 chapters as it dives deep into the trauma, mental illness, and addiction that required the miracle that happens in chapters 10-12. Settle in for a slow burn because the end is worth it.

The point of my story is to convey a message that a pastor gave me when I was at my worst, and it is this: "God is, God hears, and God delivers." I am writing this story to put hope on display for people in situations that seem hopeless. Hopeless cases are God's specialty.

# INTRODUCTION

*"For you created my inmost being; you knit me together in my mother's womb." (Psalm 139:13, NIV)*

Someone once told me that if you cannot remember your early childhood, it's likely that your childhood was a good one. I am not sure I agree with that, but I have difficulty remembering much of my childhood before age six. I experience brief flashes of memory, but the context of those memories is hazy. I suppose it's because I am decades removed from the events and remember them through the lens of a child. Assessing my memories, I have no reason to think that an outside observer would have viewed my early childhood as anything but good. After all, I had a mom who loved me and worked to support my sister and me. I had maternal and paternal grandparents who did positive things for us, took us places, were always happy to see us, and I had exposure to aunts and uncles that seemed to care. I even knew six of my eight great-grandparents. I also had friends that I played with in my neighborhood, at church, and at school. I had suffered no abuse at that point and had encountered no tragedies, yet I recall something in the world (or in me) felt off. For reasons that I cannot fully explain, the world didn't feel entirely safe. I was an outgoing, loving, and energetic child, but I engaged the world with a sense of unease. I lived with what I can only describe as a persistent anxious hum somewhere unknown deep inside of me. I existed, and I wasn't entirely comfortable with it. Even as a young child, perhaps as young as five years old, I remember wondering about life, existence, and God in as much as a young child can think about such things.

My mother raised me in the church, which might explain why such things would be on my mind at a young age, but it was also the constant hum of unease, my unpleasant shadow-like companion that brought such thoughts to mind. Given the environment I was raised in, the general sense of anxiety I experienced cannot be explained. My early years were filled with light, but I was distracted by the hum, which made the light seem dim in my memories. Try as I might, I can only trace the uneasiness to one source: my father's absence from my life almost from day one. His absence and life choices set me on a pain-filled trajectory. The path would eventually land me in pleasant places but not before it nearly killed me. As a result, this story begins not with me, but with him.

# CHAPTER 1:

## Sins of a Father

*"Anyone who does not provide for their own relatives, and especially for their own household, has denied the faith and is worse than an unbeliever." (I Timothy 5:8, NIV)*

I was born at Edwards Airforce Base (AFB) the year the Vietnam War ended in 1975. My father was an aircraft mechanic in the military. My mother was a stay-at-home mom. My sister is two years older than I am, and my parents were still teenagers when we were born. My parents' families couldn't have been more different. My maternal and paternal grandparents lived no more than a mile from each other, but the family cultures were hundreds of miles apart. My maternal grandfather was a Special Agent of the U.S. Treasury and came from a reasonably well-off, community-involved, white-collar family in Northern California. He was a strait-laced, by the rules, God-fearing professional and family man. He had strong ideas about how people should live and tried his best to raise his children according to his principles.

My maternal grandmother was a nurse. She also came from a family of professionals. Both sides of my mother's family were stereotypical, white-collar middle class with strict Christian values. My mother, as the youngest child, was a bit of a rebel and a free spirit. I don't know if my grandparents understood her, or if they even tried. But they caused each other considerable grief. My mother ultimately rebelled against them in the form of my father. After my mother had children, she settled and grew into her adult responsibilities. My mother is an intelligent woman, but I think that having children early in her life narrowed her opportunities.

My father's family wasn't nearly as educated or well off as my mother's family, but they were intelligent people as well. I would not have called them poor, but they were blue-collar working-class people. My paternal grandfather was a carpenter, as were his brother and father. The older men in the family taught my father and uncle carpentry skills, and eventually, they both joined the Air Force. I recall my paternal grandmother working various jobs as a child. She was a skilled seamstress and was very artistic like her parents. There seemed to be problems in my father's family, but I could never quite put my finger on the source.

My mother told me that my paternal grandfather was distant, restrained, and undemonstrative when it came to his children and his own father shared similar traits. I grew up around both men and I would agree with my mother's assessment of them. My father's parents argued a lot when I was little, and it was evident that my grandmother was the dominant adult in the family. I don't recall my grandparents sharing a bed. They had different rooms and I didn't observe what I would consider love or romance in their relationship. Although I felt welcome in my paternal grandparents' home, it did not feel as warm and loving as my mother's family. There was often negativity in the air. My father grew up in this environment.

My father was a severe alcoholic, a binge drinker, who would go on alcohol benders but then would get sober and not drink for periods of time. My grandmother told me that he began coming home drunk at the age of 12. My mother later added that he had been sexually active from about the same age.

People who knew him would say that he was quiet, artistic, and charming, but he had demons, so to speak. My mother said she believed that he battled anxiety and depression, which may explain why he abused alcohol. But why so young? Nobody knows. My pattern of behavior in my preteen and teen years mirrored his in many ways, but there were known factors that contributed to my early troubles. Nobody has been able to explain my father's behavior to me. I was taught early on in counseling that when people are having problems, we should never ask what is wrong with them but instead ask what happened to them. I often wondered what happened to him. I wonder what hurt so badly that he drank the way he did.

At the age of 16, my mom became pregnant with my sister, and my parents married. Despite his alcohol problem and assumed mental health issues, my father was brilliant. He finished high school early and went into the military but was often unfaithful to my mother. On the day I was born, I was told that he called his other girlfriend to tell her he had a son.

When I was three or four months old, my father's drinking, infidelity, and sporadic violence toward my mother and sister were too much for my mother to handle. She left my father and came home to Fresno, California to live with her parents. We stayed with my grandparents for a short time until they bought us a little house in the neighboring city of Clovis, close to Tarpey Elementary School.

Due to its proximity to Fresno, Clovis has been described as a wealthy suburb of Fresno, which is partially true, but the area around Tarpey Village, where I grew up, didn't follow the Clovis stereotype of affluence, white-collar workers, and successful business owners. Tarpey was brimming with low-income families, many of them single parents, many more with problem kids. Too many of those children are dead today because of drugs, alcohol, or other forms of violence. Neighborhood relationships I formed in the 1980s contributed to my early initiation into alcohol and drug use, early sexual activity, and crime. I will discuss these later.

My mother tells me my father would try to see my sister and me periodically. I remember he almost always left shortly after we arrived at my grandparents' home. He also tried to reconcile with my mom, but he would not give up alcohol or other women.

I don't remember much about my father, and it wasn't until I began writing down my story that I realized none of the memories that I do have are positive. I recall eating with him at a fast food place around the corner from my grandparents' house. We were walking home on a busy street, and, for some reason, someone yelled at him from a car. He yelled back, flipping off the driver, and threatening him. I also have memories of him drinking and driving with me. Another time, he was driving me back home to Clovis from my grandparents' house, and we ran out of gas. He only had some change, so he went into a 7-Eleven store, bought a Gatorade, took a drink, poured it out, and then filled it with gas when the store clerk wasn't looking. I remember confronting him about it and he told me to not tell my mom. One time, he came to our house in Clovis, which was rare, and fell asleep on the floor. I wanted his attention and bothered him when he was sleeping. He woke up, spanked me hard, and sent me to my room. I remember feeling so angry, that I punched my bedroom door and screamed. I just wanted him to pay attention to me because I rarely saw him. When my parents took us places together, he seemed to focus on my mom and not his kids. I have other sporadic memories, but they are not much better.

I always wanted to see my father and longed for his attention, but he also made me feel nervous, as did his friends. He must have been charming because everyone I have spoken to who knew him, seemed to like him.

When I was four years old, my parents divorced. My father went to Korea for a year. I was too young to know what "going overseas" meant. I didn't understand what Korea was. I only knew he had left. He did write me a letter, and I remember him sending my sister a Korean doll and me a soccer ball.

I didn't know this at the time, but during my father's time in Korea, he killed a Korean national in a bar fight and was arrested and imprisoned. My family later told me that it was an accident. During that time in Korea (1980), there was an attempted coup, the Gwangju Uprising, and the Air Force was able to get him out and send him home.

When he came home, his drinking escalated significantly. I would see him at my grandparents' home periodically, but my mother kept us away from him as much as possible, and I was angry about it. I was even angrier that he didn't make much effort to see me.

Like most boys, I idealized my father. But like many substance-dependent parents, he made promises he didn't keep. It didn't take me long to determine that we were not his priority.

Most people who knew my father agree that whatever it was that hurt so bad inside of him was compounded by the guilt of having killed a man while he was overseas. He was reckless even before the alcohol-induced spiral that ensued after he came home from Korea. My mother told me that he was in a motorcycle wreck that almost killed him, and another time he took out 600 feet of chain-link fence with his car on his way back to Fresno from Edwards AFB. My mother also told me someone stabbed him at some party and when he went to the hospital, he got belligerent with the doctors and decided to go home and just put Band-Aids on his wounds. My aunt (his sister) said to me that at some point, he had seen a therapist who told him he was a ticking timebomb waiting to go off.

I know my father only through these stories. The picture that forms is of a hurting person who learned to soothe his pain with alcohol and sexual promiscuity. The alcohol and sex solutions became problematic and resulted in the neglect of his children, multiple failed marriages, reckless behavior (resulting in personal injury and property damage), the death of another human being, and prison all by the time he was 26 years old.

People told me some good things about my father growing up, but as an adult, looking back, I think they didn't want to tell me the whole truth about him because they didn't want me to think less of him. Perhaps, they didn't want to believe the truth about him either. I don't like to think that my father was a horrible person. My later life wasn't stellar either and followed many of the same patterns, so it would be hypocritical of me not to recognize that. I know that hurting people hurt people but my father, like all of us, had choices. He made many poor choices that had far-reaching consequences for me, my sister, my mother, her parents, and his parents and siblings. Both sides of the family told me he loved my sister and me, but there was no evidence of that. If he loved me, I never felt it. He was young, in pain, and addicted. Perhaps, he couldn't have shown love to us under the circumstances, or perhaps he could have but chose to avoid his responsibilities. We will never know what a healthy David Prichard could have looked like, but one thing is for certain, he failed at being a husband to my mother and a father to his children, and that failure had massive ripple effects in the lives of people around him.

# CHAPTER 2:
## When Darkness Descended

*"The human spirit can endure in sickness, but a crushed spirit who can bear?" (Proverbs 18:14, NIV)*

It was a beautiful spring morning in April of 1982. I was six years old, and my sister was eight. For some reason, I remember that morning well. My mom told us we were going to my grandparents' house. I remember walking out the front door of our house and climbing into the car. It was sunny, the air was cool, and the sky was clear. It felt unusual that we would be going to my grandparents that early. Something felt off. When we got there, my grandparents didn't seem like themselves. The atmosphere felt sad.

My mom sat my sister and me down in the living room. My grandparents sat across from us. I can't remember what my mom said exactly, but she eventually told us that our dad had died. The oxygen left the room like someone kicked the wind out of me. I cried, riding the waves of anger and sadness which hit at the same time. My mom and grandparents were also in tears. My sister sobbed uncontrollably and at some point, left to go into the kitchen. Our mom went after her. My grandparents stayed with me. I remember the sorrow on their faces, but the rest of the day is a blur. I find it odd that I have no memory of the day that changed my life forever. A live grenade might as well have exploded in the room that day, and in a way, it did. I still live with shrapnel from that explosion in my soul, and it aches. That single event was the catalyst for everything that transpired in my life after that time, and for the next 25 years, my life went dark.

I would later learn that my dad was shot and killed entering a neighbor's house in the early hours of the morning on April 7, 1982. Apparently, he was intoxicated and headed from a party to his parents' house where he lived. The house my father was killed in was only two streets over from where his parents resided. It's believed that the owner of the house left his keys in his car and the car unlocked. My dad may have been so intoxicated that he thought it was his car and passed out inside of it. In any case, the theory is that he stumbled home drunk from the party, passed out in the car, came to, grabbed the man's keys he found in the car, and entered the house. When he did, the owner shot and killed him. The toxicology report said my father's blood-alcohol level was 0.24, which is very intoxicated. A blood alcohol concentration this high would likely result in confusion, trouble with motor coordination and drowsiness.

A few days later, my mom asked my sister and me if we wanted to go to the funeral home to see him. I believe she thought we needed closure. She had consulted with a therapist who had recommended she do this. My sister refused to go, but I went. I recall walking into a dimly lit building. My mom then led me deeper into an even dimmer room.

As I walked in, I saw the silver casket straight in front of me. To the left, stood a picture of my dad and his service flag folded up in a triangle box on a wall shelf. My mom stood toward the end of the casket by his feet. He was wearing a dark brown suit, and he looked like he was sleeping. I reached my hand into the coffin and touched his hand. He was so cold and stiff. I looked up at my mom and said, "Momma, why is he so stale?" I remember my mom trying to explain that this is what happens when we die.

I think the therapist was partially right. That day it became real. I needed to see it. I needed to touch him one last time and know he was gone, but it didn't give me closure, not by any means. My dad's death made no sense to me. I was full of anger and sadness, and it later exploded out of me in every direction, toward my family, peers, adults, and all authority.

People thought I was angry at my dad, and I was, but I was also confused and scared. His death destabilized me internally. I was raised with a Christian worldview that teaches that God is in control of all things. So, in my mind, my father's death was God's doing. The church also said God was loving and caring but, taking my dad from me didn't feel loving or caring. It felt like a betrayal. I believed in God, and I couldn't unbelieve even if I tried, so all I could do was blame Him. Also, if God would take my dad from me, what else was He willing to do? I was scared I could lose my mom as well. I remember listening to sermons at church and I wondered if God even liked people because God seemed so random and angry, always punishing people. God scared me.

The anger, defiance, and rebelliousness that came out of me toward others were born in this confusion, uncertainty, and anger towards God, who took my dad from me. I didn't ask to be born and I raged against it. I only see this clearly looking backward. I had no idea what I was feeling at the time. At its core, all the problems that I would have later in life were rooted in existential angst pertaining to God, and it was fueled by my father's early neglect and sudden death. This is where the story really begins and ultimately ends, with God.

All I had of my dad were my few memories and stories people would tell me. They were stories of pain and bad behavior. I needed him but he was never there for me and now couldn't ever be. My hope was gone.

The death of my dad increased the uneasiness I had always felt in the world. I believe fathers, and to some extent mothers, affect our ability to relate to the idea of God. It isn't hard to understand why our views of God are so distorted because even the best fathers are flawed. Without a father, I was adrift with no anchor, and God, who took my father from me, couldn't possibly be a loving father.

My mom later told me she had to peel my sister out of the car at the cemetery on the day of the funeral. She didn't want to go. My mom also told me that my behavior was very bizarre. I only recall sitting on my grandmother's lap in front of the silver casket. People were crying. I was numb. After the funeral, I remember running around the graveyard, jumping on people's headstones like I didn't have a care in the world.

I didn't feel sad that day or shed a tear. I was hyperactive. I became acquainted with the cemetery that day though. It became a place I would regularly go to at night as a teenager and young adult. Many of my darkest hours were spent there at night just laying on my dad's grave, talking to him, or praying to God. I think I was looking to connect with my dad, searching for answers that could never be found there. The only connection I had to my dad was his bones under the ground where I would lay.

Sometimes I would grieve and express anger, and other times I was acquainting myself with the reality of death because I knew it would eventually come for me. In a way, it was a comfort that I would be with him in time, and perhaps that is why I behaved so recklessly in my own life. Touching my dad's cold hand that day colored the way I saw the world, my place in it, and other people, and coupled with my religious upbringing it made me view God with anger and fear. I'm not being overly dramatic when I say that death and eternity became the themes of my life. My dad came to represent the uncertainty of life and the certainty of death, and God represented judgment and eternity. These themes invaded my soul.

My mom later told me that I changed after my father's death, and I remember feeling different. My sleep was interrupted by bad dreams. I became extremely defiant with adults, especially my mom. I fought constantly with other kids and was disruptive everywhere I went. I didn't care about school. I played with kids in the neighborhood when they were available, but it's hard to keep friends when you're so aggressive. I remember experiencing deep periods of sadness mixed with nervous energy and anger. I was different from other kids. I saw the world differently.

I think the adults around me just saw a hyperactive boy with some behavioral issues that he would probably outgrow. I now believe my behavior was a manifestation of significant trauma(s) and, perhaps, child bipolar disorder or cyclothymia. Whatever the ultimate causes were, my moods were often dark. Explosive anger, defiance, and violence became my default behavior in response to stress.

My dad's death created identity problems for me in his family as well. My mom believes that my dad was the favorite child. He was doted on, at least by his mother and his grandmothers. One time, my mother told me she asked my grandmother why she loved my father more than her other children, and she said, "I don't love him more; he just needs me more."

My grandmother used to tell me that my dad's brother, my uncle, was her sturdy oak, the strong one. She said my aunt was her rose, but my dad was her African violet and needed a lot of nurturing. His death was hard on the family. As his son, I inherited the favored status. My grandmother and great-grandmother doted on me as they had him.

I look like my dad, and people in my family mistakenly called me David and not Michael. This happened regularly. My identity on that side of the family was tied to him, and I internalized it.

Looking back, I am not sure that they loved me solely for me or because of my connection to their lost son. But either way, I felt loved. My grandmother spoke about my dad a lot, but often my grandfather avoided me. His interaction with me was shallow. I think he may have felt guilty about not being a better father to my dad, but I can't say for sure. Perhaps seeing me all the time didn't help. He wouldn't talk to me about my dad, so I never knew his true feelings.

# CHAPTER 3:

## Early Wounds

*"But you, God, see the trouble of the afflicted; you consider their
grief and take it in hand. The victims commit themselves to you;
you are the helper of the fatherless." (Psalms 10:14, NIV)*

After my dad's death, nothing was the same. At the time, I was
enrolled in a Fresno school close to my grandparents' houses so I
could walk to their homes after school. I hated going to school, had
no interest in doing work, had trouble making friends, was always
in fights, and was defiant with teachers. I was often in the principal's office. I hated listening to other kids talk about their dads. I
dreaded Father's Day. The other kids making gifts for their fathers
only reminded me that mine was gone and there wasn't a thing I
could do about it. For some reason, I felt ashamed that I did not have
a dad. I made gifts for my grandpa instead.

To make things worse, I was bullied at school by older kids. I
recall one incident where one of the older kids on the playground
kicked me in the stomach so hard that I dropped to the ground and
almost threw up. One bully was constantly pushing me around and
threatening to hurt me.

I often woke up with knots in my stomach, knowing my day
would consist of hated schoolwork and attempting to avoid bullies.
I also feared that I would do something that would land me in the
principal's office. I wasn't always able to control my angry outbursts.

After school, I avoided the bullies on the way to my grandparents' house. If I'd gotten in trouble that day, I sat in anxiety, waiting for my mom to get home. I had one teacher that would rate my behavior on a scale from 1 to 4. Every day she wrote numbers on a small piece of paper and pinned it to my shirt so my mom would know how I did that day. I never felt like the teachers or school staff cared about me.

If the report from the school was bad, my mother would be angry. She yelled. A lot. I was a problem child and often felt like I was an inconvenience.

I never told anyone about the bullying. I was embarrassed and I had slowly learned to not trust adults. I don't think anyone had a clue I marinated in anxiety all day long and suffered from depression. Things were about to get even worse for me.

The fences in our neighborhood were low and kids often jumped over them to each other's houses. One day, I was jumping fences and noticed a teenage boy had put up a big colorful tent in the backyard. I remember asking him what he was doing. He said I could come to look inside. I was nervous because he gave me the creeps, but my curiosity got the better of me. I climbed the fence and walked into the tent. It was empty. He zipped the tent from bottom to top. My heart beat double time. I tried to jump and reach the zipper, but I was too short. I asked him to let me out. He told me if I wanted out, I had to suck on something. I had no idea what he meant, but I was scared enough to do what he said. He made me lay down, close my eyes, and open my mouth. He hovered over me and forced me to perform oral sex on him. I was frozen. I didn't open my eyes. Thankfully it did not last long.

He got up, told me I could open my eyes, and unzipped the tent. I could see him walking away, trying to zip up and buckle his jeans. I climbed the fence in shock. I felt so violated and literally sick to my stomach. I also felt shameful and weak as if I had done something wrong. I was afraid if I told my mom, I would be in trouble. I was always doing things that got me in trouble. That day, my innocence was taken from me, but it wouldn't be the last time that I would be sexually victimized. Between the ages of 7 and 9, there were more shame-producing secrets for me to keep. Subsequent sexual abuse happened about a year later in my maternal grandmother's neighborhood.

I was an active kid, the stereotypical rough and tumble boy. My mom felt that it was important for me to have that freedom since I lived with all females and my dad was not in the picture. Being adventurous, I all too frequently encountered the neighborhood group of teens and none of them were good news. These were the kinds of kids that encircled younger kids and forced them to fight older, stronger kids. I was a younger kid.

One day, they made me fight another older kid in the neighborhood. I fought to the point of exhaustion and was beat up badly. After the fight was over, one of the teens brought me ice water, but they loaded it with salt because they thought it was funny.

One thing these kids had, and I didn't, was a bike. Even at the risk to my physical health, I couldn't stay away from watching them build and jump ramps. One teenage boy in the neighborhood invited me into his home. The movie *Toys* was on the TV in the living room. After talking to me for a while, he grabbed a plastic bag from a box stashed under an end table. It contained half-smoked marijuana joints. At the time, I had no idea what they were. He pressured me to smoke with him, but I felt very uncomfortable. I did smoke it, but I don't recall ever feeling high. He showed me around the house, but when I got to his room, he tackled me on the bed and threatened to beat me up if I didn't perform oral sex on him. I was 8, and he was 15. Even so, I resisted, but the threats got worse. I knew he would hurt me, so I thought I would just do it and get it over with. It felt like he made me do it forever.

To make matters worse, during the act, he called a girl on the phone and talked to her. Once again, I left feeling violated, guilty, and sick to my stomach, but also a little more desensitized than the first time. After all, it had happened before. I was used to holding secrets at this point, and I had no one I could tell. It was too embarrassing to talk about anyway. I was becoming numb. I just did what I had to do to get through the moment and then tried not to think about it, but the world felt very dangerous to me and there was more to come.

My mother wasn't rich. As for many single parents, daycare was an issue. A family near one of my grandparents' homes agreed to watch me. I sometimes visited my grandma during the day when I was at the sitter's house, but I don't know why she didn't watch us.

This family, especially the parents, were very religious and I recall never feeling comfortable there. But it wasn't the parents that generally watched me, it was their daughter.

One day, she pulled me into her room and told me that she loved me. It felt weird. I think I innocently told her I loved her too. After all, she was nice to me. She repeated that she really loved me and then hugged me tightly. I didn't fully understand at eight years old, but it didn't feel appropriate. Other babysitters had never hugged me like that. After I left her room, I left the house and walked down the street, feeling anxious, like I was bordering on having an anxiety attack. Later, I came back to the sitter's house, laid down in the living room, mind racing, but finally fell asleep. I wasn't the type of kid to nap. I was distressed and was trying to escape reality.

That day began my early lessons in sexual contact with a female. Hugging progressed to romantic kissing. Romantic kissing led to adult touches. She taught me adult sexual terminology and how to touch and kiss her all over. Soon, touching turned into oral sex.

At this point, you may be wondering why I just didn't tell someone. The truth is, I was scared of my mom because it seemed, from my young perspective, that I was always in trouble, and I knew this was wrong. My sister and I didn't get along and I felt she hated me, the school staff were figures who doled out discipline, not protection, my father was dead and my grandparents, as good as they were, reported everything to my mom. God was a punishing distant figure in my mind. I had learned to fear and hate authority. I was alone. Alone with secrets too big for my young shoulders.

To add another layer of shame, in the beginning, I was very uncomfortable and scared; but, because I am heterosexually oriented, I grew to like some aspects of our relationship. She showed me the attention I craved and didn't threaten me.

But my feelings of guilt escalated. I had even more secrets from my mom. She had spoken to my sister and me about sexual propriety at a young age. I'd been raised in the church. I knew what we were doing was wrong. This sexual abuse lasted for months but finally ended.

It was in the fall of that year when God first interjected himself into my story in an experiential and personal way. My mom took me to a service at church on a Sunday night. Sunday night church was the norm, but there was a special speaker that night. He was a magician of sorts. He had this little Rolls Royce car that he drove onto the stage, and he pulled huge objects out of it. I mean, this car was tiny. At the end of the act, he pulled his wife out of it. It was amazing. I don't remember a word he said during the show, but I loved the tricks.

After the act was over, he preached about God's love for us and how He sent His son Jesus into the world to save us, but we needed to ask God to come into our lives. He then asked if there was anyone who wanted to come up front, pray and ask God to come into his or her life. I felt a tugging inside of me to go to the front for prayer. I was hurting and burdened with shame and guilt. I know beyond any doubt that God was calling me to the front. I finally got the nerve to get up and go. I recall crawling over the people to get into the aisle to go up to the alter. I stood there with one older adult, and I knew everyone was looking at us, but I didn't care. I started crying as he began to pray for me. I didn't fully understand what was happening, but I felt that God touched me in a deep place within. I felt God's presence and knew that God was aware of what had happened to me and how bad I was hurting, and He responded with His presence. I felt that tug at my heart again and again throughout my life as God showed up to meet me in my pain.

Even though God showed me love in this way, I still feared Him because of the hell fire and brimstone preaching of the church I was raised in, but I believe that day God marked me out as His own. I felt adopted. At the time, I understood God as much as an eight-year-old could understand Him. The long-term effect of that initial encounter with God didn't manifest itself until much later in life, but as I began to study the Bible as an adult, I learned God cares for widows and orphans.

Before I move on to the next part of the story, I need to say more about how being sexually abused negatively affected me long-term. The molestations by the male figures made me feel weak and vulnerable. I hated that feeling. I was tired of being bullied and victimized by people. I learned young it was better to be the aggressor than the victim because it's not always possible to hide.

As I grew into my teen years, being a bully was a form of self-protection. Aggression is how I eventually learned to deal with threatening male figures.

The effects of the molestation of the female figure had a different impact entirely. The weight of the secrets and the guilt were heavy to carry as a child.

I was taught in church that any sexual enjoyment had one proper context: marriage. I knew what we were doing was wrong. Even at 8, I knew this kind of thing should not happen with a teenage girl. But because I enjoyed some of it; I didn't feel as much a victim as a participant. It felt good. I liked feeling good. I knew this was wrong. This struggle produced a whole new level of guilt.

The sexual experiences with this female informed the way I viewed intimacy with females for a long time. I had become sexualized. I already had trouble relating to peers, but except for the women in my immediate family, I could only connect to females in sexual terms. I had lost the ability to develop wholesome relationships with girls and developed poor boundaries with girls my age.

Even though I desired to have relationships with girls my age, my behavior put them off and the relationships did not last long. Later, this led to me having sexual relationships with older girls. It wasn't until my early twenties that I began to see women as people with feelings and not just sexual objects. Inappropriate thoughts and behaviors toward females really began to manifest at about the age of ten (4th grade) and the beginning of my twenty-year addiction to drugs and alcohol started around the same time.

# CHAPTER 4:

## Blended Chaos

*"If a house is divided against itself, that house cannot stand."*
*(Mark 3:25, NIV)*

In fourth grade, when I was 10, I transferred to attend Tarpey Elementary School. Tarpey is in Clovis Unified School District and was very near my house. The kids who attended were from my neighborhood. Clovis is known for the quality of its schools. They also are very big on athletics.

I had hated the school I was at in Fresno, and I don't think the teachers were very fond of me, so I was looking forward to a new start.

My behavior improved a little because of the change in atmosphere, but I brought all my issues with me and Clovis seemed to have little tolerance for troubled kids.

Beginning in the 4th grade, Clovis kids are offered a variety of athletic opportunities. I tried everything. I wasn't too fond of cross-country or football but wrestling and track events called to me. I won field events in track and made varsity wrestling my first year. I never walked away from a wrestling tournament without a metal. I loved sports. I also liked the girls that went to Tarpey, and some of the girls seemed to like me. I had little cheerleader girlfriends, and life was better at Tarpey. But my grades were terrible, mostly because I would never do my homework. I loved to listen and learn. I paid attention in class much of the time, but I didn't want to do the work.

Outside of school, I loved to skateboard. On the weekends, I begged to spend the night with my grandparents so I could skate with the older kids in their neighborhood. We hung out at the mall together. We were all considered social misfits and got along well.

My mom was hesitant to allow me to socialize with these kids, who she assumed were a bad influence on me. We frequently fought about it. I was acting more defiant, and she didn't like it.

Around this time, my mom began to date a man who attended our church. We'd gone to that church for years, but I don't recall ever seeing him before they began dating. I liked him right away. It was apparent that other church members liked him as well. I wanted a dad, and he seemed like a good guy, but I already had issues relating to a father figure so as much as I wanted a dad, the reality of our relationship proved difficult.

My mom began to be firmer with me in terms of discipline and I knew that this new man was in her ear, giving her directions. He grew up with a strict Christian mom where kids were expected to act a particular way toward their parents and if they misbehaved there were physical consequences. I acted up a lot, but this sudden hardline my mom took with me was foreign and unwelcome. I blamed her boyfriend. My mom didn't know how to handle me, so she looked to this new man for guidance. As far as he was concerned, she was the parent, and I was supposed to obey, but neither looked deeper into the reasons for my behavior.

Hardline punishments never worked with me. I was too angry, and they only increased my anger and caused me to resent my mom. Her boyfriend continued to encourage her to turn up the disciplinary heat as my rebellion escalated. I already felt my mom had betrayed me by always taking the school's side. The trouble that happened at school wasn't always my fault. My mom's participation in viewing me as a problem kid made her feel unsafe to me and as a result, I couldn't talk to her. I needed a caring safe zone.

One day, my mom and I were fighting about something. She had a switch in her hand and swung at me and, although that isn't what she intended, almost hit me in the face. I was so angry; I took a swing at her but missed. She walked out of the room.

It's hard to explain the confusion that happens in a child when they love their parent and are desperate to be understood but they carry so much resentment and anger that they push that same parent away. In my mind, as a child, my mother should have been on my side, but I felt she sided with everyone who was against me instead. I often felt that she was embarrassed by me. To some degree, I think her father may have made her feel the same way. All my mom saw in me was out-of-control defiance.

Later that day, this man, who wasn't my dad, came into the room and pushed me down on the bed. He grabbed me by my neck and threw me up against the wall and threatened me. He said he would have done worse if he was my dad.

I couldn't believe my mom allowed this man, who was not my father, to treat me that way. Nobody knew what I had been through or what I was feeling, and nobody inquired. I now felt bullied at home. I wanted a dad in my life but only had an idealized version of what that meant. This was not it. I was hoping for something else. I wanted a friend, an ally, a support.

Looking back, I wonder if my behavior could have been modified if he had tried to befriend me and spend time with me. I needed someone I could talk to and be honest with. I needed someone who could mediate between me and my mom. I know now that kids respond to trauma in different ways. Some kids detach, some experience depression and anxiety, and some act out with aggression. Kids that act out with aggression have difficulty finding advocates. This is what happened in my case. There was no advocacy for Michael.

Right after this incident, I began emotionally detaching from my mom. She was still my mom, but I couldn't connect with her. Something changed in me. I was confused. She told me she loved me but what was happening in my home didn't feel like love. It felt like frustration and anger. Also, what love and attention I did receive from her began to shift to this new man. I never did reconnect with her completely. I was approaching my pre-teen years and the window for healthy parent-child bonding was ending. It wasn't all her fault. We had all been through a lot. She was young and ill-equipped to deal with traumatized kids and there was more trouble to come.

It was also right after this incident with my mom's boyfriend that I started smoking cigarettes daily. I had used tobacco a few times before, but I didn't like it. This time it served a purpose. For a few minutes at a time, it calmed my anxiety. Within a very short time, I was smoking 5 or 6 times a day. By the time I was almost 11, I was a half-a-pack-a-day smoker. Tobacco wasn't hard to get. My mom was a closet smoker, so I stole them from her. I also stole them from friends' parents, and I had adults buy them for me. One store knew my mom and would sell them to me sometimes if I lied and said they were for her, and at that time restaurants had cigarette machines that were accessible to anyone.

That same year, I spent the night at a friend's house who was a little older than me, and we snuck out to a jr. high/high school party. I got drunk at that party. This was my first experience with alcohol, though I had already smoked marijuana a time or two with a friend in my grandparents' neighborhood. At 11, I was on my path to addiction. I didn't care for marijuana, but I loved alcohol. It made my anxiety and depression disappear for a while.

The summer I turned 12, my mom and her boyfriend went to Nevada to get married. I don't remember being told they were getting married, but that week my grandfather took me to a Christian camp called Calvin Crest. I didn't want to go. I'd liked it when I was little but now, I had nothing in common with the Presbyterian kids. I spent my free time alone and went off to smoke or chew tobacco. I do remember goofing around in an empty cabin with some other kids a few days into camp. I had a stick and broke the light bulb. They accused me of vandalism. When they also found out that I chewed tobacco, they called my grandfather to come and get me. He was a pillar in his church and wasn't happy. I asked him to drop me off at my paternal grandparents' house so I could wait until my mom and new stepdad got home. I knew I would be in trouble.

This was the incident that earned my first beating from my new stepdad. He grabbed a thick switch and gave me a little lecture on why this was a Biblical form of discipline and how he had the responsibility to do it. He beat me so hard I had bruises from the back of my neck all the way to my calves.

The Bible does describe discipline as a *rod* (Proverbs 13:24) and some Christian denominations take that literally. In as much as kids are capable of actually hating their parents, I hated my mom at this point. I couldn't believe she approved of this. Because she didn't know what to do with me, she delegated the responsibility of discipline to my stepdad. As I stated before, this type of discipline was part of his upbringing. I don't think he knew another way.

It was obvious, even to me, that he didn't enjoy punishing me. He seemed to feel bad, but he felt he had a responsibility to do it based on his religious beliefs. Other than his brand of punishing discipline I received, he was a good guy in all other respects. I do not blame him. The churches that endorse this type of severe discipline are wrong. It's never appropriate to beat a child or leave bruises.

A few days later, I had a track meet at school. The teachers saw all the bruises and asked me what happened, so I told them. School officials are mandatory reporters and while they did call Child Protective Services (CPS), my mom later said that they told her they waited several days until the bruising went down so my parents wouldn't get in trouble. Even Tarpey staff knew the severity and the potential consequences of what had happened. The school was aware I had behavioral problems. Given my behavioral problems, perhaps the staff at that time thought I deserved it, or that perhaps somehow a beating would fix my behavior. It didn't. It made things worse. When CPS was alerted, they interviewed my mom and stepdad but not me. Looking back now, I am glad my parents didn't get in trouble, but the school and CPS missed an opportunity to get me and my mom the help we so desperately needed.

At the beginning of my sixth-grade year, I was kicked out of Clovis School District for fighting. There was too much going on too fast. My mom moved my sister and me out of the only home we had ever known to a house with my stepdad and his two sons, where we didn't have our own rooms. I loved the home I grew up in. My grandparents owned the house so after we moved out, I would spend time there by myself until it was sold. The two stepsons who came with the marriage were also not entirely kind to my sister or me. The younger son didn't like this new blended family any more than my sister and I did and often showed it by making mean comments. At this point, I checked out completely, and so did my sister. I didn't feel like I had a place in this new family.

In writing this story, I wanted to be careful not to cast my mother and stepfather as villains. They weren't. They were caring parents, but even caring parents can make mistakes. They just operated within a firm conviction of their belief system. They were completely ignorant of all the abuse I had suffered. I just looked like a rebellious, out-of-control child, not a hurting one. They did as best as they could with the tools and knowledge they had available to them. In retrospect, I don't think either of them would say that their hardline approach with me was a healthy way to discipline, but we can't live our lives in retrospect, only learn from our mistakes.

My mom didn't know what to do with me. My stepdad felt like he had an obligation to help my mom and disciplined me according to how he was disciplined. They loved us and treated us well overall and tried to make things as pleasant as possible, but blended families are not easy, and their kids were not happy.

There was only one other incident of physical punishment shortly after I turned 12, but much less severe than the first one. I honestly think my stepdad felt bad about what had happened before.

The truth is, I needed and wanted a dad. I called him dad right away, despite it all. People wanted me to behave and fall in line, but I was as confused about my behavior as everyone else. I was always in trouble, and there were consequences, but I still couldn't get it right. At a young age, I had no way of understanding that unresolved trauma contributed to my feelings and behavior, and I really couldn't see how my choices would result in long-term negative outcomes. I was impulsive, angry, and easily triggered. I didn't know what was wrong with me, but I started to view myself as a problem because everyone else seemed to. I absorbed the labels people put on me.

There was more to my stepfather than the way he disciplined me. As I grew up, he became a huge support for me, even more than my mom at times. He had his own issues before he became a Christian, so he was often more patient with me than my mom. He just hated lying and defiance. He grew to love me and took his responsibility to us seriously. He was a good man, and I grew to love him. These early incidents of hard discipline in no way encapsulate the amazing human being he was throughout the rest of my life.

But I couldn't express the anger building inside me without risking punishment and so I dealt with it in other ways. I stayed away from home, used tobacco and alcohol, and talked to girls on the phone. The family never did blend entirely.

The rental we were all living in was too small for us, so my parents moved us to Madera Ranchos. Madera is the county north of Fresno County. The house was way out in the country. It was big but not fancy. It looked like a long mobile home on a few acres. Since Clovis kicked me out before my 6th-grade year, my parents decided to put me in Fresno Christian Schools for 6th grade. It was like attending daily Church camp. I hated it. There were pretty girls there, and that was the only reason I could endure it. On the weekends, I stayed with my grandparents a lot of the time so that I could hang out with friends at the mall.

I wasn't skateboarding much anymore, but I hung out with mods and Wiccan people at the Fashion Fair Mall. Not all were kids. One guy was in his twenties and had been raised in the occult. He often spoke to me about it. I have always been fascinated by anything spiritual and spent a ton of time in Walden Book Store reading about it. Even though God scared me, the stories of the Bible fascinated me as well. My mom had read them to me from the time I was a child. I believed in spiritual things, and this was a new thing. I began to buy and read everything on the occult I could get my hands on.

When I was in class at Fresno Christian, I doodled these occult symbols on my notebooks and talked about them with others. This got me in trouble. To me, it was just another school that didn't like me. I didn't fit in. I didn't want to go to a Christian school anyway. The staff there, like at the other schools, didn't take the time to talk to me or understand what was happening behind the behavior. There were expectations and kids that didn't meet those expectations didn't get to stay.

I didn't care. Other than talking to girls, I felt that school was a waste of time. After one semester, and a fight with another kid, Fresno Christian kicked me out. They told my mom I could never, ever return.

I enrolled at Webster School in Madera. This was an elementary and jr. high school. I didn't like it any better. Webster's saving grace was that it had a wrestling team, and the coach had just moved next door to us. He took an immediate liking to me because I was a Clovis wrestler. Clovis is known for producing some of the best wrestlers. I wanted to wrestle again, and I did. Even with my smoking and drinking, I went undefeated and won the valley championship. I beat a Clovis wrestler in the finals, which satisfied me greatly since they had kicked me out.

I was so good that my coach enrolled me in jr. high school tournaments when I was still in elementary school. I did reasonably well, but like always, I didn't do my work, and my grades eventually impacted my ability to participate in sports.

I found ways to drink and get tobacco in Madera, but it was harder, so I continued to stay with my grandparents when I could. My grandparents didn't always like me there either, but I pushed them to let me stay because I wanted to drink and hang out at the mall. At this point, I was hanging out with gang members at the mall.

I hung out with so many different groups during my teen years and took on so many false identities, I often felt like an actor putting on costumes for various roles. There were two reasons for this. First, I had no sense of myself. I seemed to fit in nowhere. Second, I needed older people to buy me alcohol.

At home, things were not going well. My stepbrothers were Clovis jocks, and even though I enjoyed some sports, my sister and I were not. We frequently fought with our stepsiblings. I think all of us were frustrated. There was so much tension in the house, that it just finally boiled over.

My younger stepbrother made wisecracks at us all the time. One night, he went too far, and the confrontation escalated into a physical fight. He was bigger than me and grabbed me from behind. I took a pencil off the counter and stabbed him in the leg a few times. My stepdad came unhinged. He'd had it with the fighting and bickering. He threw all the cooking dishes and dinner off the counter and yelled at all of us. When it was over, his finger bled from a wide gash, and there was glass and food everywhere. Everyone retreated to their corners.

He and my mom were trying to create a happy home life for everyone, and it wasn't working out the way they had hoped.

I know there must have been times when my parents wondered if their marriage had been a mistake. I was miserable at home. I wanted out. I remember at one point; I took off from the house and called the local sheriff.

I knew a deputy who patrolled the area. He was nice to the kids in the Ranchos, but he's not the one that came. When this other deputy showed up, I told him I wanted him to take me away from my family - I wanted to be a ward of the state.

The deputy drove me home and spoke to my parents. Apparently, he had a child who ended up being a ward of the state. It was a desperate cry for help on my part, but only resulted in me, once again, in trouble with my mom and stepdad and gave my stepbrothers more fuel to ridicule me.

By the end of summer, going into my 7th-grade year, I was an alcoholic. Although I didn't drink every day, I managed to get drunk several times a week. I often drank alone. I craved the oblivion of alcohol constantly.

When I didn't have alcohol and wanted to get high, I huffed paint. I used to huff paint until I passed out. I don't know how I still have a functional brain.

The consequences I suffered from my alcohol and drug use were worth it to me until my wrestling coach wouldn't let me on the team because he found out I smoked. He also wouldn't overlook my poor grades.

Shortly after I found out I couldn't wrestle, an 8th-grade boy picked a fight with me and knocked me unconscious in the scuffle. Once again, the school administration determined I could no longer attend their school.

My parents were very angry. I had to go on home studies to finish out my 7th-grade year. However, without the school environment as a distraction, my grades improved.

My parents owned a small construction company, and, at this time, it landed some significant jobs. Money began to come in. We were all tired of living in Madera, so my parents purchased a home in a nice area of Clovis.

Just like that, I was headed back to Clovis schools. Clovis was my stomping grounds. It was my cradle, where I felt most comfortable. My biological dad was buried there. I was raised in Clovis, and I was happiest there. I was excited to go home, and I had hope that things in my life would improve.

# CHAPTER 5:

## The Story of Two Sick Children

*"As fish are caught in a cruel net, or birds are taken in a snare, so people are trapped by evil times that fall unexpectedly upon them."*
*(Ecclesiastes 9:12, NIV)*

Having a new house, a fresh start, and being back in Clovis had a positive effect on our family. Everyone's mood improved. All that summer, I stayed with my grandparents or at friends' houses so I could drink and mess around with the girls in the neighborhood. I still hung out with gangs at Fashion Fair Mall while at my grandparents, but as I entered my 8th-grade year, the appeal began to fade.

I approached Clark Intermediate School with mixed emotions. I was glad to be back in Clovis, but I didn't know anyone, and I was still dealing with all my anxiety and fear. As much as the move felt good, it was still a change and only amplified those anxieties. It was stressful.

I quickly made a few male acquaintances, and of course, I never had trouble interacting with girls, but some mornings I downed NyQuil before school to keep my anxiety in check. Of course, I then had a hard time staying awake in class.

I didn't have the social skills to interact with normal kids. I wasn't unpopular, but I didn't have a lot of close friends. The best part about being back in Clovis was I got to wrestle again. I had traded smoking for chewing tobacco, so my lungs were in much better shape.

The wrestling coach taught my homeroom classes. That year I went undefeated in wrestling - nobody could touch me. I won all the local tournaments. The one thing that brought the family together was sporting events. My stepbrother and stepdad came to some of my tournaments, and I appreciated that.

I excelled at wrestling, but my grades suffered. The principal informed me I couldn't go on to the State Championship unless I pulled up my grades. The principal didn't seem to care much about athletics, but he did care about my grades. He offered to tutor me at school until 8 pm during the week and then drive me home. I hated having to do schoolwork until late in the evening, but I'd never had anyone take a real interest in my learning potential. Even though I had to miss wrestling practice for a month, I was able to bring my grades up and go to the State tournament.

The last match was close, but I won the State Wrestling Championship. When I called home to tell my family, my stepdad was really happy for me. But what I remember most happened near the end of the year at 8th-grade graduation. The principal gave me a special award for the most improved student, and he told the parents and students how hard I had worked to get to the State Championship. I also won the coach's award for wrestling, but I almost cried when I was called up to receive the Principle's Honoree of the Year Award. I had never been honored or recognized for anything academic, and the award took me by surprise. It's still in my office to this day. I wonder sometimes what would have become of me if adults in my life would've taken the time to help me reach for higher goals and had shown me the difference one adult can make in a child's life. I believe that principle has passed now but I will never forget him.

While everything was going better for me at school, we had a catastrophe at home. My youngest stepbrother was diagnosed with an aggressive form of leukemia. The news shook our family. He was

18 years old and an avid bodybuilder. He had a dream to be Mr. California. My older stepbrother played college football in Montana at the time. Everything changed in the house. My stepbrother began chemotherapy and was always at Saint Agnes Hospital. His mother worked in some high-level position for the State and couldn't take leave to care for him because his insurance was through her work.

My stepdad worked out of town, building hotels in northern California. He came home on the weekends and spent most of his time at the hospital. My mom also frequently stayed with my step-brother, making sure he wasn't alone. Despite our family's rocky moments, she loved him as though he were her own.

My sister and I were frequently on our own. My mom made sure we had money and food, but supervision was rare. I was still drinking, and at this time I became sexually active. Because I had been sexualized as a child, it was the only way I knew how to connect with females. At age 13, older females began to show a sexual interest in me. I jumped at the opportunity. Women became a comfort zone for me just like drugs and alcohol.

During the summer before my freshman year, I suffered from severe depression and intense anxiety. I couldn't figure out the cause, and it was overwhelming. It may have been the uncertainty in the home, but I am pretty sure I just naturally had mood instability. I didn't cope with it very well as an adolescent. My mom began to worry about me, but she was dealing with my stepbrother's illness. He was physically sick, while I was mentally and emotionally sick.

My mom had to deal with problems on multiple fronts, but because my stepbrother had a serious physical illness, understandably the family's attention was focused on him. Mental health wasn't as well understood back then, so I became sicker and sicker. I experienced crippling sadness, lethargy, and irritability in the extreme and I was a chronic drinker. I thought nobody really saw what was going on with me, but despite the unintentional neglect surrounding my substance abuse and mental health issues, God saw what was happening. As was His pattern throughout my life, He appointed people to help me.

The lady next door to us did manicures from her home. She did my mom's nails a few times. She and her husband were also pastors. He was from a Russian community, and she was from Tennessee. I liked her accent and her sweet tea. My mom communicated what was going on with me, and this southern woman took me under her wing. She took me to church, taught me the Bible, and assigned me scripture to read. She had me read the book of Proverbs, and I loved it. Proverbs was all about pursuing life wisdom and the value of wisdom. I was fascinated, and it gave me hope that there was a kind of wisdom that would make life better. I asked God for wisdom constantly, and as I pursued God my depression began to lift.

This woman spoke words of life to me regularly and acted as a spiritual mother for a time. I felt God's call on my life once again. I needed this, especially as my family became less available. For a brief time, I began to view God in a positive light without fear. I stopped drinking.

About three months into my freshman year, I became involved with a female at church, and it ended badly. As I began to get to know the people attending church, I saw the problems in their lives and began to lose respect for them. They were not the icons or role models I wanted them to be. I stopped going to church and I started drinking again.

Once I left the church, I stopped visiting my neighbor. I lost all accountability. In my freshman year, I made new friends who further drew me away from Christian morals and females began to show me even more attention. I just gave up on all my spiritual pursuits and my depression and anxiety returned.

During my freshman year, I nearly cut my thumb off with a bandsaw in 3D design class. I had to have the nerves in my thumb micro-stitched back together. The doctor gave me oxycodone (brand name Percocet), and I loved it. When I took this drug, all anxiety disappeared, and it elevated me out of my depression. Needless to say, I ran out of it quickly. Shortly after, I had my wisdom teeth pulled out. That dentist gave me hydrocodone (brand name Vicodin) to deal with the pain. I loved that as well. I'd discovered a new kind of drug: prescription opioids. I decided I wanted more oxycodone. I had already learned to lie to get alcohol when I needed it, so I told my mom the hydrocodone made me sick and asked her to get oxycodone from the dentist. They gave it to me, and then I had two prescriptions.

After those ran out, I couldn't stop thinking about and craving opioids. I was obsessed. I got them wherever I could, usually from other kids who had prescriptions. Around that time, my stepbrother's doctor prescribed him oxycodone for cancer-related pain. I stole them all the time. The cravings only increased. I couldn't stop myself.

One time, my brother got a new prescription, and in four days, I had taken 60 of them. I denied it, but my family knew. I had to find other ways to get them because, at this point, I viewed them as a necessity. I went to the bookstore and purchased a Physicians Desk Reference (PDR) to learn about all the drug classifications. I memorized all the scheduled drugs by their brand names, chemical names, and manufacture, so I knew what to look for when I rummaged through people's medicine cabinets. I did this everywhere I went.

Opioids were way better than alcohol - they were my drug of choice. Even though opioids are technically sedative compounds, they stimulated my thinking. I took them, waited for them to take effect, and then read books. I wouldn't just read any books, I read college-level anatomy textbooks, the PDR, textbooks on psychology and philosophy as well as religious books. I did horrible in school because I didn't want to do my work, but I loved to learn. I listened in class and read on my own. I was full of information that was essentially useless at my age, but my interests were never the same as others around me. Despite my private interest in knowledge and the fact that I was reading and comprehending college-level information, Clovis High School put me in low-level classes because of my failure to do schoolwork.

My stepbrother went into remission about a year after he got sick, and everyone was hopeful. He slowly gained his muscle back. In fact, he got bigger and stronger than he was before he got sick. But his cancer came back sometime toward the end of my freshman year. This time he had to go to the University of California San Francisco Hospital. My mom and stepdad were rarely home. My maternal grandmother came to stay, but she was no real supervision.

My depression came and went, but then I started experiencing elevated and irritable moods and depression. These moods occurred even when my substance misuse was minimal. It felt like an emotional rollercoaster. We have a history of mental illness in the family, and our doctor diagnosed me with bipolar II and generalized anxiety. The doctor placed me on lithium and an anti-depressant. I stabilized while I was on it to some extent, but I kept drinking and using drugs periodically. I had a substance abuse problem, severe mental health issues, and family troubles, so I didn't wrestle in high school. I look back on this with sorrow today. Who knows, if things had been different, maybe I could have been a four-time state wrestling champion for Clovis High School.

When I was on my medication, my grades came up and my mood improved, but they made me feel mentally slow and fatigued and gave me a dry mouth. I hated the side effects, so I just stopped taking them. Within a few days, I began to experience insomnia and extreme anger. I lashed out at teachers, students, and others around me. I couldn't control it. I was so agitated that my mom took me to the ER. Hospital staff placed me on a 5150 hold and admitted me into the Renaissance psychiatric facility at Clovis Community Hospital.

Before I was taken upstairs to the hospital, I stole a bunch of alprazolam (brand name Xanax) from my mom's purse in the ER. I swallowed the pills when she wasn't looking. I was then escorted upstairs to the locked-down facility. I don't recall the first day because I had taken so much alprazolam. I was only there for three or four days, but the psychiatrist confirmed the initial doctor's diagnosis and put me back on medication. I was fifteen years old at this time.

After I got out of the hospital, the psychiatrist who treated me continued to see me for my bipolar disorder, generalized anxiety, and ADHD well into my 20s. The doctor didn't fully comprehend the severity of my addiction history and prescribed me abusable drugs. In addition to the lithium and anti-depressants, he gave me benzodiazepines for anxiety and prescription amphetamines for ADHD. I took the prescriptions within a few days and then would drink, find pain killers, and I eventually used meth in between when it was available.

I began my first real relationship going into my sophomore year. She was a freshman. I met her leaving a football game when I was a freshman and she was still in eighth grade. Although I became infatuated with her immediately, I wouldn't go out with her when she was in jr. high school. We spoke on the phone from time to time and she visited my house that summer.

I am not sure why, but I felt that she was different from other girls. The relationship put me through emotions that I couldn't handle. I was emotionally unstable anyway. I didn't know how to have a real relationship with anyone, let alone a female. I was the very definition of selfish and she was a sweet person. I felt deep affection toward this girl but I was insecure and jealous. Over our two-year relationship, I didn't treat her well. Looking back, I can say I was abusive.

I viewed women as sexual objects and was very promiscuous. I wasn't kind to any woman for many years. I hurt people and that isn't pleasant to remember. My substance use and mental health issues became worse that year, and I attribute it to my inability to deal with my own negative feelings, the careless prescribing of drugs that increased my substance addiction, and the emotional impact of my stepbrother's illness on the family.

# CHAPTER 6:

## Death in the Family and the Aftermath

*"I have seen something else under the sun: The race is not to the swift, or the battle to the strong, nor does food come to the wise or wealth to the brilliant or favor to the learned; but time and chance happen to them all." (Ecclesiastes 9:11, NIV)*

One morning, in the September of my sophomore year, I woke up and my room was already hot. My window faced the sun, and it glared into my room. I glanced at the clock and it read 10 a.m. Why hadn't anyone woken me up for school? I threw on a t-shirt and walked out of my room to the top of the staircase only to see all our close family friends in the living room below, sitting there with their heads down. I thought perhaps they had all come to pray for my brother, which was a normal thing in our home but when I went downstairs into the den my mom and stepdad told me that my stepbrother had passed away early that morning at the hospital. They had decided to let me sleep in.

I turned around and walked upstairs to my room. I needed to get out of the house, so I got dressed and went to school to tell my best friend and girlfriend what happened. I was in shock; I couldn't believe it.

We belonged to a church denomination that believes in miracles. For years, people had been coming to our home to pray for my stepbrother. We believed God would heal him. Some of these men that came to pray for my stepbrother claimed to have gifts of prophecy and healing. They had told my family that God would heal my stepbrother.

After he died, we never saw or heard from those people again. I believe God can and does speak through people and does miraculous things, but I have met many people in the charismatic denominations who claim to possess gifts and abilities they don't have. I think they believe in their own giftedness to the point of delusion and, in the process, give people false hope. I call this religious narcissism.

Our family was devastated and confused. My stepbrother's death shook everyone to the core. My stepdad was hurting; his faith in God shaken. My oldest stepbrother was deep in grief. My mom had exhausted herself taking care of him and trying to manage the family. She began to fall apart emotionally. My sister kept her feelings close, so I am unsure how she felt, but my drinking and drug use escalated and so did my mental health issues.

My stepbrother's death brought back all my insecurities about God and who He was. There was a deep sadness in the home, and people were disengaged from each other. My stepbrother and I were five years apart. We had not gotten along very well at times, but I was pulling for him to get well. During his illness, God got ahold of his heart, and I think it humbled him and everyone else in the family. He became a gentler and kinder person.

I had already faced one major death in my life, and I hadn't been around my stepbrother his whole life, so his death didn't have the same impact on me as it did on my stepdad and stepbrother. We were all expecting him to make a recovery. It was shocking that God would suddenly take him while I slept that night. He was only twenty-one years old.

As I already stated, that year, after my stepbrother died, my mental health seriously declined. I think I was wrestling with doubt about God and the meaning and purpose of life. I was sad about my stepbrother's death, but our family dynamic changed for the worse as well. I was no longer using drugs and alcohol for the high, but to escape the changing circumstance of my life.

I was never good at identifying my feelings or working through them. My emotion meter had two settings: good and very bad. My meter rarely tilted in the direction of emotionally good naturally, so I used drugs to try to force it in that direction.

One weekend I scored a lot of meth and took too much. My heart began to have arrhythmias, and I had severe chest pain. I suffered through it for several hours before I woke up my parents. My mom rushed me to the ER at Clovis Community Hospital. My heart was racing so fast that it didn't feel like it was beating at all. The ER doctor gave me high doses of propranolol to slow my heart. He told me I was lucky because he had lost kids my age to stimulant overdose.

Later, an echocardiogram revealed a conduction problem on one side of my heart. The doctors said I might have been born with the condition and the meth had made the problem worse. My parents knew I had issues with drugs and alcohol, but the meth overdose made it more real. I think my mom was scared and angry. My heart's rhythm was off for some time. I was scared I would die. My mom stayed up with me at night to make sure I was ok, but I could tell she was irritated with the situation, and she was worried about me. I quit using meth for the time, but I was still drinking, using opioid pain killers, and dealing with mental health issues.

About a third of the way through my junior year, I found out some guy at school had come over to my girlfriend's house and gave her a ride in his car. I had serious jealousy issues when it came to her. I wanted to hurt this person. I took a knife to school the next day. The school staff found it in my locker. I was immediately expelled for having a weapon on campus and had to be on home studies for the rest of the year.

That was the beginning of the end of my relationship with my first girlfriend. It had never been healthy, but the relationship grew toxic. I don't blame her at all. The drugs, cheating, mental health issues, and abusive behavior were too much for anyone to handle. I was becoming increasingly unstable.

I began to have persistent thoughts of suicide. Not only did I suffer from periods of deep depression and chronic, crippling, anxiety, I had intermittent episodes of mania. This wasn't a happy mania; it was angry agitation. Right before my girlfriend and I finally broke up, I recall telling her I wanted to kill myself. I don't think it had as much to do with our relationship falling apart as it did the fact that I couldn't find happiness in my life anywhere.

She was staying with a friend that night, and her friend told her grandma I was in danger of hurting myself. The grandma called Clovis PD and they came to my house. I was outside in the front yard, out of my mind on drugs, when Clovis police drove up and approached me with their hands on their guns.

My mom came out of the house and told the police I would be fine at home and that they could leave, but the police were hesitant to leave me alone with my mom because I was acting so erratic.

I was distraught when the relationship with my girlfriend finally ended, but I buried my pain and focused on another girl. I was out with an acquaintance one night, and he wanted to go see a girl but she had a friend with her, so he dragged me along. I didn't want to go but I needed to get more beer anyway. When I met this girl, we hit it off immediately and stayed together for many years. She was beautiful and smart, and from a family of well-known educators in Clovis. She was way too good for me. I don't know what she saw in me or why she put up with me. She liked to party a little and have fun, but she wasn't addicted to alcohol or drugs like I was.

When I was feeling well, I was a fun person. I am affectionate and loving, but people got hurt when I was not well, and she was no exception. As much as I liked this girl, I was still emotionally on and off with my first girlfriend and saw other girls as well. I think she knew, but I lied about it. For the most part, I didn't have casual relationships with other girls because I liked them. They were sources of drugs and alcohol, which was always priority number one. Also, female attention made me feel good about myself. When I was young, I was angry and very insecure. My emotional insecurities bled into all my relationships but most strongly affected the young women who cared about me the most.

At 17, the drugs and alcohol were no longer working to help with my emotional discomfort. In fact, now I had to use drugs and alcohol just to stave off withdrawal symptoms. I finally asked my parents for help.

My mom took me to a rehab in Clovis called the ARC. At that time, there were no adolescent programs providing medical detox for kids my age in my area. I was the only adolescent in that place, and it wasn't an appropriate facility for me. One of the counselors told me that it was a rare thing to see someone in my condition so young. He commented that it had only taken me six years of using drugs and alcohol to bottom out.

The program offered me nothing useful except medical detoxification. I had to attend adult groups and couldn't relate to the discussions. During family counseling, the counselor asked my mom to tell me about how my addiction made her feel. My mom looked at me and said, "Sometimes, I wonder if you even love me at all."

Her comment hurt me deeply and made me very angry. I was voluntarily getting help because I couldn't control my drug use and she made it about her. I felt as though she were saying, "Michael, your love for me should be enough for you to just spontaneously get better."

She had no idea what I had been through or the depths of my addiction. I had made choices that led to my condition, but there was no insight or ownership on her part as to how some of her actions and other family problems might have contributed. Once again, my mother seemed to view me as a problem to be solved.

This seemed to be the story of my life. It wasn't just true about my family, but it was true of my teachers, church leaders, and adults in general. Who was I supposed to turn to? With later insight, my mom probably needed therapy as much as I did. We had been through so much and our relationship was damaged. I loved my mom but was very angry and resentful toward her at the same time. I think my mom's feelings toward me were reciprocated.

I stayed in rehab for two weeks, but my insurance ran out. My maternal grandfather wanted me to come and stay with him. He thought he could make a difference in my life. I stayed clean for thirty days but eventually started drinking and going to doctors to ask for prescriptions of abusable drugs. I had blackouts and couldn't remember things that I did. One time I was cooking food in the microwave and just passed out on the floor.

I would stop breathing in my sleep from all of the opioids and benzodiazepine drugs. My body would jerk itself awake, I'd gasp for breath, and felt tingly like I was oxygen deprived. I called poison control on myself several times in the same week, and a woman at the call center told me I was addicted to these drugs and needed help.

One time I went to a walk-in clinic to try and get drugs. I had been there once before, and they had prescribed painkillers to me. I am unsure how the medical staff knew to call my mom, but they kept me waiting in the exam room for an hour and then directed me back out to the lobby where my mom confronted me. I was furious with the staff and I was furious with my mom for interfering.

I stormed out of the office and headed back to my grandfather's house. I didn't feel well enough emotionally to cope with life. Drugs and alcohol were a necessity. I treated them like any medication but even I knew they were killing me. Any attempt to deprive me of the only things that relieved my discomfort set me off.

Eventually, my grandfather called my mom and told her that he couldn't handle me there at his house. She had warned him, but he didn't listen to her.

My paternal grandparents had moved to Idaho to be around my uncle and cousins. My mother explained the situation to them, and they all agreed it might help to leave California. I didn't want to go. It felt like my mom was trying to get rid of me.

When I got to Idaho, I was an anxious, nervous wreck. My cousin told me that they sold codeine cough syrup over the counter in Idaho, so I bought a bottle to calm my nerves and drank the whole thing. My cousins were younger than me, but one of them knew where to get alcohol, so I was able to drink. My uncle made an appointment with a psychiatrist who prescribed me alprazolam for my anxiety. I drank and took the medication. Within a week, I was in the ER because of a bad reaction to alcohol combined with my psychiatric medication.

One of my cousins told me my grandfather said that I was just like my dad. This wasn't true; my addiction was worse. I remember thinking that maybe it was my grandfather's neglect of his son and poor parenting that contributed to my father's problems and the reason why I had to grow up without my dad.

In my addiction, I was no different than many other addicted people. I placed blame on others for my problems.

Being in Idaho was a bad experience for many reasons, all of which were my fault. After the hospital incident, my grandparents sent me back home to my parents. I know my mom didn't want me back.

When I got home, I continued to drink and hang out with some guys I knew in high school who partied all the time. It didn't take long for me to be in trouble at home, but I had learned not to care.

My friends called me one night and told me they needed my help because they were going to fight a group of guys near where my girlfriend lived. We went to Clovis Bicentennial Park to find them, but they weren't there. My girlfriend's house was near the park, so some of us started walking into the neighborhood toward her house. Right as we turned the corner onto her street, the other guys jumped out of a car. One of them had a big steel piece of a car bumper jack and ran at me. I ran around the corner and saw a flatbed truck with a bunch of 2x4s. I grabbed one of the 2x4s and ran back around the corner to meet him. As he raised the piece of steel in his hand, I hit the guy in the forehead and cut his eye open. They all ran. The cops were called and they were looking for me. I had turned 18 when I was in Idaho, so now I was an adult. I figured Clovis PD just wanted to question me, so I went to the station. They arrested me. I was taken into custody and placed in a holding cell.

On the way to the holding cell, I passed the guy I hit and could see the cut on his head. He just glared at me. Oddly, when I turned myself in, Clovis PD didn't search me. I don't even recall being placed in handcuffs on the way to Fresno County Jail. When I got into the booking area in the jail, I took out an empty can of chewing tobacco I had in my pocket. It contained 5-6 extra strength hydrocodone pills and three 2mg alprazolam pills. The officer asked what they were, and I lied and told him they were my psychiatric medications. He didn't question me but said I should take them before I was booked because he didn't know how long it would take for me to get my medication in the jail. I swallowed them all. By the time I was taken to psychiatric housing, I was high as a kite. In high doses, alprazolam always blacked out my memory, so everything about that experience is hazy, but I do recall getting into a confrontation with a bunch of other guys in the jail pod and I had to be transferred to another pod. I was there for three days but my girlfriend talked her mom into bailing me out. I was charged with assault with a deadly weapon but when I went to court, they deemed it self-defense. The other guy was convicted and given probation.

Going to jail didn't change my behavior and my parents were tired of me. I had nowhere else to live so they pressured me to go into Teen Challenge.

# CHAPTER 7:

## Sober Discontent

*"For who knows what is good for a person in life, during the few meaningless days they pass through like a shadow?" (Ecclesiastes 6:12 NIV)*

Teen Challenge is a well-known Christian recovery program that helps people overcome addiction to alcohol and drugs and other life problems. It began with a pastor working with gangs in New York City. Substance use disorder (SUD) is a medical diagnosis and so modern alcohol and drug treatment is based on a medical model. But when Teen Challenge was founded, there were only social model programs and church-based help for the addicted. Social model programs come from 12-step recovery movements, but churches developed their own recovery-oriented programs based solely on Biblical principles.

Many people have been helped over the years by faith-based programs, but these programs are not for everyone. Teen Challenge is associated with the Assemblies of God church denomination. This is the denomination I grew up in, so the program's culture wasn't foreign to me at all. The denomination is one of the many referred to as Pentecostal.

I showed up at Teen Challenge shortly after I turned 18. My girlfriend drove me to Shafter (near Bakersfield, CA) and dropped me off. I think she had mixed emotions about me being gone for a year, but I also think she knew I needed help. She had been through a lot with me.

I hated Teen Challenge right away. It was a little ranch in the middle of nowhere. There were guys there from various walks of life, but most were on the bottom rung. Out of about a hundred men, I was the second youngest.

I snuck in drugs and tobacco in the lining of my jacket, but they ran out very quickly. The staff let me take my psychiatric medication in the facility, providing it when needed. I did get stable. I was bored there though. There wasn't a thing to do except pray, go to Church, do chores, and read the Bible. Perhaps that is what I needed. I wrote my girlfriend and when I went home on a medical pass, I got to see her. I was feeling better after a few months and resolved to stop using drugs and drinking. However, right as I was beginning to acclimate to the program, I got into a fight with another guy.

I remember I didn't like this guy. He was obnoxious and probably 10 years older than me. We were in our dorm, and I was talking to some other guys when he suddenly popped off at the mouth. I hit him twice and blacked his eyes. I was called to the office, but on the way there, he ran up and hit me from behind. We were both kicked out and I had to go home right before Christmas.

My parents were angry and told me that after the 90-day waiting period, I was going back. Well, in that interim, I found out my girlfriend was pregnant. Of all the things I didn't want to discuss with my parents, it was this. I didn't like talking to my mom especially. At times she was calm and supportive but most of the time she was reactive just like her father had been with her.

I kept taking my medication when I left Teen Challenge and wasn't using any drugs or alcohol. I was feeling better, but I still had to see a psychiatrist because there was no way I could stay clean and sober unless I stayed on my medication.

One day, my mom gave me a ride to see my psychiatrist. During the appointment, I told him that I was going to be a dad. He asked if I had told my mom and I said that I had not told her. He strongly encouraged me to bring her in from the lobby to tell her.

My mother had firsthand experience with having children young. I expected a negative response or a lecture at least. That isn't what happened at all. After I told her, she kind of softened toward me. I think she was excited about a baby coming.

My parents still insisted I attend a program but instead of Teen Challenge, I went to a local men's home called the Harvest Home. I was relieved that I got to be there for my girlfriend. I was excited and nervous about the idea of being a dad, but it motivated me to do better.

Harvest Home was associated with Bethel Christian Center in Fresno and it was the first church I remember attending as a little boy. Many of my earliest childhood memories were associated with it. My biological father's grandparents, parents, aunts, and uncles had gone to this church. The pastor's wife had led my mother to the Lord, and the pastor counseled her and my father when he was still alive. I had deep roots there. I loved the pastor. I learned more under him than any other pastor I'd known. I have had bad experiences with pastors in various churches, but this pastor was the genuine article. It was evident that he loved God and lived out his faith. While I was at this men's home, I worked at the church part time and then rode my bike across town to Clovis Adult School several days per week. I eventually completed high school in the program. I then enrolled in Fresno City College.

My son, Gabriel, was born on Halloween 1995. His mom wasn't thrilled his birthday was on Halloween, but I thought it was the coolest thing ever. I had just turned 20, about the same age as my dad when I was born. I was so glad I was clean and sober to welcome him into the world. My father couldn't say the same. I remember standing in the delivery room and the nurse handing me scissors to cut his umbilical cord. She then wrapped him in a blanket and handed him to me. I nearly had a panic attack. I felt dizzy. The weight of responsibility became real. Before, he'd been more or less an abstract concept. Now he was real. I didn't know what to think or feel. I carried him into the nursery, where his grandmothers had their faces pressed against the glass, waiting to see him. There was so much excitement in the family around his arrival. I loved this little boy with every fiber of my being. I wanted to be a good dad and I was hands-on with him. I took my son everywhere with me. His mother loved him to pieces as well and both sides of the family spoiled him. He was the first grandchild. Everyone loved him but my stepdad had a special bond with him.

After the program, I kept going to church and finished some classes at Fresno City, but I didn't do well in college. I wasn't disciplined enough. My stepdad took me to work with him and had me clean up job sites. I did small things around the office, and while I got a check from my parent's company, I really didn't do much to earn it. My parents were trying to help as best they could. They were not going to have their grandson go without anything.

But even with the son, who I loved more than anything, I struggled with unhappiness. I hated the side effects caused by my medication, but I had to take it to stay stable and not relapse. The medication helped me make sound decisions. My biggest issue has always been compromised emotional states. On the medication I still suffered from depression but, at least my moods were somewhat manageable. Even so, I felt like a broken human.

All of the psychiatrists that I have seen in my life told me that bipolar people require lifetime medication, but looking back, I am not convinced that my diagnosis was entirely correct. How can doctors diagnose a person as having a mood disorder when that patient's alcohol and drug use imbalances the brain in a way that causes mood instability? I had also suffered a lot of emotional traumas that were left unaddressed.

I spent all my time with my son. I wanted him to know he was deeply loved because I hadn't felt loved by my father. I also cared for his mother, and now that we had a son, I knew she wouldn't tolerate a relapse.

My parents pressured my girlfriend and me to get married. They continually reminded me that I didn't want my son growing up, knowing his mom and dad were not married.

When my son was 18 months old, we married, and his mother enrolled in college. I knew she was smart because I never won an argument with her, but I didn't know she was academically inclined or that she had goals. She wanted to be a scientist, and she achieved it. She eventually earned two master's degrees and went on to get her Ph.D.

Yet, I had no direction. I was just lucky to be sober. She married me anyway. I thought being married and trying to be a good parent was just a normal societal expectation. I wasn't motivated to achieve much beyond that during our marriage. This was a source of frustration for my stepdad, who saw my potential. He used to tell me, "You are the smartest of all of us and you are throwing it away." What he didn't understand is that it doesn't matter how smart a person is if they cannot control their mental health issues.

Religion and politics were major points of contention in our marriage. Arguments arose over how we would raise our son. We fought a lot, and eventually, she decided she wanted out. I didn't. I was scared because even with our differences, she helped anchor me in my sobriety.

Other than the fighting, I know I had hurt her a lot throughout our relationship. I hadn't been nice to her. I had been unkind and often unfaithful before I got clean and sober, and I am sure it was hard to forget.

In the end, she had goals for her life and didn't let anything keep her from them. We separated a year after we married, and my life began to deteriorate though it didn't show immediately. I was nearly 23 years old.

During our marriage, my wife and I had been going to a Bible study. A new girl had shown up a few weeks before I announced my wife and I were getting divorced. A friend in the group told me she had asked if I was married. Since my wife resolved to divorce, I keyed in on this girl. I felt so angry, hurt, and rejected that I began seeing her before moving out of the apartment I shared with my wife. I needed a new anchor, but this girl couldn't be that for me. She didn't have the historical context of my drug use or mental health struggles. My wife knew me better than anyone. She had been through all the troubles with me over the last six years.

When my wife and I separated, I moved back to my parent's home. There were no child custody issues. I saw my son as much as I did before. I was seeing this new girl, but I was grieving over the split with my wife. I still didn't know how to process intense emotion.

My new girlfriend had a lot of good qualities, but my family didn't care for her. They were pleasant, but they didn't think she was for me. They also loved my son's mother and didn't want to see the divorce happen in the first place. I was so self-absorbed; I was oblivious to how they felt.

Shortly after I started dating the new girl, United Parcel Service (UPS) hired me part-time. I felt that I was on my way to a better future; my life was getting on track. At least in the short term. I was wrong.

# CHAPTER 8:

## Relapse

*"As a dog returns to his own vomit, so fools repeat their folly."*
*(Proverbs 26:11, NIV)*

After five years clean and sober, I'd forgotten how miserable addiction had been. My wife and I were still separated. Although she insisted that she wanted a divorce, she'd never taken the final step. I'd made a few attempts to reconcile, but she wasn't interested. I eventually filed for divorce later so that I could remarry. I still had my new girlfriend who I'd met at Bible study and eventually, my wife began to date another guy.

My new girlfriend and I began attending a little house church that a friend at the Bible study told us about. I connected with the minister at this new church and had become excited about the things of God again.

The pastor knew we weren't married and suspected that we were in a sexual relationship. He was concerned because he knew that I had a spiritual calling on my life. He confronted me about the nature of my relationship with my girlfriend on multiple occasions. I knew I wasn't living consistent with my beliefs, but I got defensive. One time he looked at me and asked me what I was going to do on the day when I had to face God. I believed in God deeply and believed that we would all have to give an account of our lives to God.

Earlier in the story, I mentioned I was afraid of God. Like the pastor, I knew I had a calling on my life, and I really tried to do better, but as time went on, I began to make compromises in my life. Seemingly small steps led me to a place I didn't want to go back to. I began to drink beer while out on dinner dates with my girlfriend. The alcohol use became more regular, but nothing I couldn't explain away. Then I found a bottle of hydrocodone shoved in the back of the kitchen cabinet in my girlfriend's house and I took them.

Opioid pain killers were my drug of choice, and the pills I found woke up the craving monster in my brain. Pain killers were easy to get at work. People had them or knew people who had them. I had excellent medical benefits at UPS as well. Eventually, I was jumping from doctor to doctor to get prescriptions. I'd even asked people I knew to get them from their doctors, and I'd buy the drugs from them. Sometimes, when I was desperate, I resorted back to my old tactics of stealing them from people or going to walk-in clinics.

My drug problem was back. I hid the severity of the issue from my girlfriend, and this produced a lot of guilt. I had been with this girl for about a year and eventually wanted to marry her.

We'd begun going to a different church by that time, so I decided to go to the pastor and confide in him about what was going on. The pastor asked if my girlfriend knew about the problem. I told him that she didn't. The pastor insisted that if I wanted to continue my relationship with her, to even marry her one day, I needed to be honest. Honesty was not my strongest quality, evidenced by the fact that none of these pastors knew that I was legally still married to my son's mother.

I knew he was right, but I dreaded telling my girlfriend. I remembered how confrontational my mother and even my son's mother had been with me. I wasn't looking forward to a repeat. When I finally got up my nerve, I went to my girlfriend's work and sat her down. I told her I was addicted to opioid medication. I remember how ashamed I felt. I waited for the ax to come down.

She was gentle with me. Part of it was probably her personality type, and the fact that she may have loved me, but I also think she was probably naïve to the realities of addiction and what it could mean for her future if she stayed. She chose to remain in the relationship.

I cared for this woman, but I went through periodic doubts about staying in the relationship long-term. We broke up several times and saw other people, but eventually, we got back together and married. After we married, my addiction progressively worsened.

If I had a steady stream of opioids, I could still manage to work, spend time with my son, and keep some semblance of normalcy in my marriage, but I was tired of going through withdrawals and always seeking out drugs. I wanted to stop the cycle.

My son's mother and I didn't spend a lot of time together, so she didn't notice I was using. My mother may have suspected but I was working and trying to be a parent and husband, so she didn't pay much attention at that point.

I appeared functional, but I was struggling. I visited the local addiction doctor who detoxed me during my first rehab at the age of 17, hoping I could stop on my own with some outpatient medical assistance, but I couldn't do it. The doctor wanted me to attend 12-step meetings at his office and I would never go.

This addiction doctor tapered me off opioids three times. I was an early recipient of Suboxone (a drug for opioid addiction) when it first came out, though it didn't work well for me. Tapering off the opioids wasn't too difficult with medical help but there were still persistent cravings for the drugs after I'd tapered off. It was this craving for opioids that fueled my relapses, as well as the fact that I wasn't taking my psychiatric medication consistently.

My, inability to cope with stress and live life on life's terms always led me back to drugs and alcohol. Like so many other addicted people, I was under the impression that addiction was just an issue of physical dependence. I thought, that if I could get through the withdrawals, I could quit. I was wrong. Opioid craving was unrelenting for quite a while after the withdrawals had ended. I could only say no to the cravings so many times before I gave in. In addiction treatment, we call this decision fatigue.

To make matters worse, the continuous high produced by the drugs reset the pleasure threshold in my brain. This means that I had to do drugs at high levels to feel pleasure at all. Natural pleasures from things like food, social interaction, and sex no longer registered when I was sober. I could no longer find joy in the things other people found meaningful unless I was high on drugs.

This brain condition is called anhedonia. It's a common condition in early recovery. Chronic substance use rewires the brain. It takes time to heal and for many people, putting time between yourself and the drug when you are addicted isn't possible without long-term treatment and support. The inability to feel normal pleasures due to chronic drug exposure, coupled with intense cravings for the substance(s), can put people in early recovery from substance use disorder at high risk of relapse.

This rewiring of the brain and the symptoms that manifest is the reason substance use disorder is classified as a chronic relapsing brain disease in medicine. With opioids in particular, I craved the high, but the emotional misery and physical withdrawal I experienced when I did not have the drug, also pushed me back toward the drug. The high was a powerful positive reinforcer but avoiding the negative consequence of withdrawal became even more critical once physiological dependence developed. Opioid withdrawal is brutal.

I think it's a common misconception that addicted people don't want to stop. Sometimes that's true, but the majority go through periods where they want to stop and can't, even in the face of mounting consequences from their use. This is the very essence of addiction. It's an inability to quit, even when a person wants to. Although a person may have made choices that led to addiction, once the rewiring of the brain has occurred, choice is rarely an option.

I had become a shop steward for the Teamsters Union at UPS and knew the business agents down at the local union hall. I finally went into the hall and asked for help. I did seek help often on my own with no other incentive but my own desire to stop. The Union sent me to rehab twice, but my sobriety was short-lived each time.

At work, there was someone I knew who sold methamphetamine. I began to use meth. I was still using opioids but used much less of them if I had meth. Meth and opioids both flood the brain with the pleasure neurotransmitter dopamine. When I was on meth, I wouldn't crave opioids because meth was an adequate pleasure-producing substitute. This allowed me to slowly taper off the opioids and avoid severe opioid withdrawal.

I had used meth when I was younger and overdosed on it, so I was more careful, at least in the beginning. Meth made work easier at first because it provided enormous energy surges. It's like rocket fuel for people, except our bodies are not designed to live in fast-forward. Long-term meth use quickly tears the body down. Meth also put me in a good mood. I felt smarter, sexual pleasure increased, and it gave me confidence.

These are some of the characteristics that make meth appealing and, in my opinion, it's more psychologically addicting than opioids. It can escalate to chronic compulsive use very quickly and in my case it did. I spent a lot of money to get it, and we didn't have much money. To sleep, I had to take prescription sleep aids because I was so amped up from the meth I used during the day. I continued to get sedative pills from various sources, and I also continued to drink.

Eventually, I was using so much meth I couldn't sleep and I didn't eat. Regular overuse of a powerful stimulant like meth, coupled with lack of sleep, inadequate nutrition, and not taking my psychiatric medication led to severe paranoia and psychotic episodes.

About four years prior, when I was clean and sober, I took up shooting guns as a hobby. I often went shooting with friends at gun ranges or in the mountains.

When I was high on meth with no sleep, this hobby became a dangerous liability. I became super paranoid. I never went anywhere without quick access to a gun. I was convinced people were after me and wanted to hurt me.

I had made enemies in my addiction, so the threat was real, but meth compounded the sense of danger a thousand-fold. I lost weight and became unreliable at work. Everyone knew I had a drug problem, including my family. I even had people pulling me aside at work to talk to me about my health.

Eventually, I told my ex-wife I had relapsed. She wasn't happy about it. She was concerned about our son. Twice, I forgot to pick my son up at school. At home, I thought my neighbors were watching me and listening to my conversations. I heard helicopters in the sky that were not there. I took the electrical plugs out of the walls to try and listen to my neighbors in the apartments around me. I stayed up all night with loaded guns, waiting to see if someone would break-in. Then at 4:00 a.m., I put on my work clothes and drove to UPS.

I didn't know this at the time, but my mom would later tell me that my wife came to her and told her about my bizarre behavior. My mom and stepdad became very concerned. It was at this point that God interjected himself into my life again.

There was a supervisor at UPS who used to talk to me about God. He was a pastor. He knew I had a problem. I had told him that I believed in God, but I was a mess. He said that he wanted to send his dad, also a pastor, to come and see me at my home. It was strange because what supervisor would risk getting involved in the life of an employee, especially when that employee is a union shop steward?

I became increasingly desperate, so I agreed and gave him my address. I had been praying a lot. I knew that I would die like my dad if God didn't intervene, and I didn't want to put my son through that.

A few days later, his dad came to see me right after I got off my shift. He was the chaplain at Chowchilla Women's Prison. When he came to my house, I was so exhausted I couldn't keep my eyes open. I vaguely remember the conversation. He could see I was in no condition to talk, but he said one thing that I remember: "God is, God hears, and God delivers."

A day or two later, I was at work, and I was convinced cameras in the building were watching me. I asked the young supervisor pastor if I was being watched. He looked at me like I was crazy. I was. I walked off the job and drove my car in a terror trying to get home because I thought every car was after me. I never went back to UPS again.

A few nights after I walked off the job at UPS, I was up on meth. I was exhausted and hallucinating. I thought someone was breaking into my apartment and I grabbed my shotgun and opened fire. The buckshot went through a wall into the neighboring apartment. My wife got out of bed because she heard the gun go off.

I grabbed her car keys and some guns and went to my sister's house in the neighboring town of Fowler. In my condition, I thought that if I took her car, I could avoid the police and other people that might be looking for me. When I returned the car the next day, I told my wife that I didn't love her. It was a lie, but I don't think she knew that. I had hoped she would leave me for her own good.

Clovis PD and Fowler PD tracked me down two days later and arrested me around the corner from my sister's house in Fowler. My sister later told me they had staked out the house. She helped them find me. I think she was afraid for me and perhaps of me. I had gotten hostile with her husband the previous day. I didn't even try and resist arrest. I was exhausted.

They took me to Fowler Police Department and Clovis PD came to pick me up. Clovis PD first took me to Community Regional Medical Center (CRMC) to have me evaluated because they thought I might harm myself. At the hospital, the police and nursing staff escorted me to an office, and I kept falling asleep during the interview. I was so out of it. They asked me questions like, "What year is it?" "Who is the president of the United States?" "Do you know how old you are?" The officer kept telling me to open my eyes and wake up. I must have answered all their questions correctly because they didn't keep me at the hospital. My next stop was Fresno County Jail.

I remember entering Fresno County Jail booking. I just fell asleep on a bench in the holding cell. At some point, the officers took me out of the cell, made me strip off my clothes, and put on a smock that barely covered my lower regions. They then placed me in a safety cell. The safety cell is an empty rubberized room. Nothing else. There was literally a square hole cut in the floor which is a toilet. I was in that room for hours. It was freezing cold.

While I was in the safety cell, I remember talking to one of the psych staff through the little metal opening in the door. He asked me what medications I was supposed to be taking and if I wanted to harm myself. I told him that I didn't want to harm myself but that was a lie. I just wanted out of the cold. I don't think he believed me anyway because officers came and eventually took me upstairs to psychiatric housing in the old part of the jail and put me in an isolation cell with a camera.

They never turn the lights off in these isolation cells, but I hid under the covers to avoid the bright lights. I was there for several days. I remember feeling so depressed. I was nutrition deprived and my brain was dopamine depleted from the overuse of drugs.

Prior to my arrest, I had gotten a hold of a sufficient quantity of methadone on the street and used the methadone to taper myself down to 10-20 milligrams per day. I told the jail staff that I was opioid-addicted and had been taking methadone. Still, they didn't help me finish my detoxification in any way that would be deemed medically appropriate by today's standards. I wasn't receiving my methadone legally from a clinic on the outside, so I had to finish kicking opioids on my own. I wasn't even medically monitored during my withdrawal. I was lucky I had been tapering off opioids or the withdrawals would have been much worse. The early stages of opioid withdrawal began to set in 36- 48 hours after my last methadone dose.

A day after I arrived, someone came to the cell door. It was the pastor that came to my house just days before. Apparently, he was also a chaplain at Fresno County Jail. I don't recall much of what we talked about during our initial meeting at my home, but now I knew for sure that God was involved. Eventually, the officers moved me into one of the pods in the old jail. By then, the opioid withdrawal symptoms had escalated. Despite the exhaustion I felt, I couldn't sleep. My stomach was in cramps, my body ached, and I had diarrhea. The stomach cramps and body aches persisted for close to 12 days, as did insomnia. Methadone withdrawal isn't as intense as heroin withdrawal, but it lasts much longer, which almost makes it worse.

After the withdrawals subsided, I began to feel better and engaged the other prisoners. I played cards and watched TV, but I was really depressed. When I called my son's mother from jail, she told me that because my son lived with me part of the time, Child Protective Services (CPS) was planning to come in and investigate the incident even though my son wasn't there the night I fired off the gun in my apartment. She told me I needed to sign custody of my son over to her to avoid CPS involvement. I was in shock. This was the last thing I wanted to do. I knew she planned to leave Fresno at some point to go to school. If I signed custody over to her, there wasn't a thing I could do to stop her from taking my son with her.

I had a day or two to think about it before the officers informed me that I had a visitor. I was hoping to see someone who cared about me. Instead, it was my ex-wife's attorney with papers for me to sign. Even though I was grieved about having to sign over custody, I decided to sign them. I knew her well enough to know that she wouldn't keep our son from me if I was doing well. Signing those papers was one of the hardest things I had ever done but I knew it was a safety plan for him. As much as I wanted to be well, I honestly didn't know if I ever would be. My son was the only thing that mattered to me. His mother would keep him safe.

My ex-wife did eventually move to San Francisco but moving there really worked out well for my son. It turned out to be a blessing in disguise.

Shortly after I had to make the painful decision concerning my son, I received divorce papers from my second wife. The papers came so quickly after the incident that I couldn't help but wonder if she had already begun thinking along those lines before my arrest. I couldn't blame her. I didn't like getting the divorce papers, but I wasn't sad about it. I wanted her to leave for her own good anyway.

While I was in jail, both sides of the family wouldn't tell my son where I was, and he wanted to know. They told him I was away getting well. So, while I didn't get to see him, I did talk to him on the phone. It was a bright light in a dark, hard time.

About a month into my stay in psych housing, a fight broke out in the pod. One of the prisoners maimed another prisoner by biting off the top of his ear. Somehow, I was implicated in the incident. The officers took me and another prisoner to a two-person isolation cell in a newer wing of the jail. I remained there for the duration of my stay while I fought the case. I believe I was in jail for almost eight months. During that time, I didn't see the sunlight. There was even a metal cover over the small window slot to the outside because a former prisoner had somehow broken out the window.

I was locked in that concrete box for seven of the eight months I was there. The District Attorney's Office initially charged me with shooting into an inhabited dwelling. In California, that's a strike charge, but it was my first offense. Because I was mentally ill and had a severe addiction, they allowed me to plea to an assault with a deadly weapon. They gave me probation and a program to complete, but I had prison hanging over my head. This felony is still on my record. The program that I was sent to was on skid row in Los Angeles (LA).

While I was still in Fresno County jail, before I left for LA, a childhood friend came to see me. I had known her all my life. Our mothers had been friends since high school. It lifted my spirits to see her. I had not seen her for years. I think she had always loved me, and I had loved her as well. We played together as children and hung out as teens but really, we were just friends during that time. I couldn't believe that she visited me. She had blossomed into an absolute angel. I wrote to her from jail and when I was released to go to the program in LA, she drove with me and my family down to LA to drop me off. We began to see each other while I was in LA but it was not under ideal circumstances for many reasons.

Skid row in LA isn't a good place to get clean and sober. It's a place where many of society's outcasts live on the street. The probation officer that recommended this place described it to jail inmates as a good dual diagnosis program for the addicted and mentally ill. He told me that the program wasn't in the best area, but from the program, I'd be able to see all the LA high-rise buildings in the business sector and make getting there a goal for myself.

As I drove into skid row with my family, I recall my stepdad saying, "Good Lord look at all the tents." It was homeless central. The program I was sent to was a beat-up, white, seven-story hotel. The fences surrounding the building had barbed wire. I was just glad to be out of jail, but looking back, it's appalling that Fresno County sent people to LA skid row, thinking they would do well there. From my perspective at the time, this program and the program across the street were poorly run social model religious programs. I cannot say if these programs were representative of all the programs in the area. I am sure some people managed to find recovery in them. In fact, I know one person who did, but during the time I was there, many clients from both programs were using drugs and sleeping around with each other and staff members. At least one person overdosed and died in the building while I was there because drugs came off the street into the program. There were a lot of people from Fresno sentenced to the program. It was as if Fresno was trying to transfer all their problems to LA.

It may seem counterintuitive to put a recovery program dead smack in the middle of one of the worst slum neighborhoods in California, but the reality is that skid row is where the most down and out drug-addicted and mentally ill people often end up. There were many missions and programs in the area that received government, church, and private donations to try to help people better their lives. While I was in the program, I met people on the streets who told me they had lived on skid row for as many as 25 years. They made it clear that they were content with it.

One of the lessons I learned while I lived in LA is that there are homeless people who want to be off the streets, while others are content to stay there. When it comes to the homeless, society seems to have one goal and that is to get them off the street. This is often done with good intensions, but other times it is simply that the living conditions of the homeless are ugly to people and it makes the public uncomfortable.

We impose ourselves on some people who choose to live this way. The homeless on the streets of skid row got food and clothing from the missions or people who donated directly to them. The homeless often have tight social networks. Many of them own cell phones. They attend religious services or 12-step meetings if they choose. Most have tent shelters and access to some level of healthcare. Contrary to what the public may think, many basic needs are met, at least in LA during the time I was there. Because these needs are met, many people on the streets are content to stay on the streets.

Skid row is a filthy, dirty place. I observed heroin and crack sold on every corner. There were stabbings and beatings on 5th street and crack-addicted sex workers turning tricks in the porta-potties placed there by the city. Despite the city's efforts, human waste littered the sidewalks. The whole place smelled like a urinal.

The program I was sent to, if you could call it that, provided housing, offered a connection to psychiatric services, and had residents do 12-step meetings. I didn't see a counselor one on one unless I was being drug tested or I had done something wrong. Many of the counselors were people in early recovery. Some of the counselors relapsed and left the program while I was in the program. I would see them on skid row using drugs again.

Once a resident passed through the initial primary phase of the program, they could wander around LA, and that is what I did. I stood out like a sore thumb on skid row. Since I was clean-cut, many of the drug dealers on the street thought I was an undercover cop. It wasn't uncommon to hear, "What's up officer," as I walked by. Sometimes if they were on their cell phone, they moved away from me. Dealers often used drug-addicted people as lookouts in exchange for drugs. They saw me coming and yelled, "Dead man walking." This was code for police presence.

Eventually, I stopped being identified as the police once they realized I was in a program, but I was far out of my element. This experience helped me see life from a different perspective and has been helpful to me in my chosen profession. I was exposed to various ethnicities of people, as well as the severely mentally ill and drug-addicted people who lived on the streets. During the time I was in the program, I learned the stories of many of the people who lived on skid row. The reason they were living on the street seemed to fall into a few categories: personal tragedy such as loss of loved ones or career, mental health issues beyond their control, and addiction. Some of the kindest and most down-to-earth people I ever met lived on skid row. They just had problems.

The program referred me to a mental health clinic on skid row, and I saw a psychiatrist who gave me medication for bipolar disorder and generalized anxiety disorder. My life in the program sort of took on a routine, at least for the first nine months. I regularly called my son and my girlfriend. I hung out with other people in the program. I loved the downtown LA library. It was massive and I could just disappear in it, which I did every chance I got, but I still wasn't happy.

LA was not home, I missed my son, and I did not blend in well in this environment.

As I progressed in the program, I earned passes to go home, see my son and hang out with my girlfriend. About eight months into the program, some guys from Fresno went home on a pass and brought meth back with them. I relapsed, but no one found out. The meth awoke the craving monster in my brain. The psychiatrist who I saw at the clinic also began to prescribed me an abusable anxiety medication. I knew I shouldn't take them, but I did. I was miserable in the program. I felt guilty about relapsing, but soon I began buying pills off the street. Hydrocodone was everywhere on skid row, but the pills were expensive. Heroin was cheaper and even easier to get. During my last three months in the program, I was using it regularly.

Heroin dealers, usually female, walked around the block of Broadway, 5th Street, Spring, and 6th Street during the day, selling little five-dollar balloons filled with heroin. People on the same block sold *outfits* or *rigs* (syringes) to IV heroin users like me. The program suspected that I was using drugs a few times, but never caught me.

I completed my year in the program, but worse off than before I entered it. I was now heroin addicted. My girlfriend and mom immediately suspected I was still using when I came home.

When I returned to Fresno, I moved in with my girlfriend. I was thrilled to see my son more and happy to be home. I began tapering off my heroin use. I used heroin periodically, but I bought opioid pain medication or methadone to reduce the amount of heroin I needed. I knew how to wean myself off drugs, but I just didn't know how to stay off of them. If I had enough lower-level opioids, I could slow withdrawal and use alcohol to calm my nerves. I was able to buy methadone on the street, so the opioid withdrawals were minimal.

My girlfriend wasn't tolerant of my opioid use at all. We fought a lot about my drug use and my lying. My drug use and our romantic involvement destroyed our lifelong friendship. Eventually, I began using meth, and the paranoia started all over again.

Things began to go horrible for me once I started using meth again. Soon after, I totaled my car on highway 41 heading home from my sisters. The accident was bad. I was miraculously not injured. It was equally miraculous that I was not under the influence. I had been up for days though and was tired coming down from the drug.

Shortly after that accident my grandfather gave me a little truck so I would have transportation. My stepdad had helped me get a job doing electrical work with one of his subcontractors. The job was south of Fresno in Lemoore. Again, I was up for many nights, I was tired, and fell asleep at the wheel. I smashed my vehicle into the back of a welding truck that stopped at a light on highway 41. I was asleep when the impact came and woke as I hit the steering wheel so hard it felt like it crushed my chest. I remember kicking open the door and falling out onto the pavement. Once again, I walked away miraculously uninjured. In my addiction, I wrecked every car I ever owned except one.

Eventually, my girlfriend and I broke up. I think she was just tired of my drug use and all the drama that came with it. I regret that it wrecked our friendship permanently.

I moved back to my parents'. At this point in my life, details remain fuzzy. I know my mom was concerned about me and probably tired of me as well. She decided to act. It may have been the multiple car wrecks that concerned her. Even though my addiction had been worse in the past, I was now wrecking vehicles, putting myself and others in harm's way.

Shortly after I wrecked my truck and moved back to my parents', I took a bunch of oxycodone and went upstairs to bed. I was so tired that it felt like I slept for two or three days straight. I woke up to heavily armed probation officers pulling me out of bed. I was naked, but I don't even remember taking off my clothes. They let me dress, cuffed me, and took me downstairs where there were a bunch more probation officers decked out in swat-style gear. I was so confused.

I was supposed to report to probation after I got out of the program, but I had thought the program put an end to my probation. On the way out, I asked my stepdad if he had called the cops on me. He said he hadn't. My mom looked at me and told me she did because she didn't want me to die.

I don't think my mom realized what would happen when she called probation. When I went to jail the last time, my mom and stepdad got rid of my guns, but my sister cleaned my room while I was gone and put random left-over bullets, gun clips, and gun parts in boxes in the closet of the bedroom where I had been sleeping. I didn't even know this stuff was there. I wasn't allowed to have live ammunition. I was in jail for about four months. When I stood in front of the judge, I found out probation took pictures of what they found in the closet, and the deputy district attorney (DA) tried to convince the judge that I continued to be a public threat and needed to be supervised at the state level. They wanted to send me to prison.

The deputy DA pursued a prison sentence for me even after my parents confirmed that I didn't know that the items were in my closet. My mom was the one who called the police and had no reason to lie, but they used the information to try and put me in prison anyway. I convinced the judge to send me to another program, but when I found out they were going to send me back to LA on skid row, I asked the judge if he was going to send me to the very place where I became heroin-addicted. Skid row, in my mind, was more dangerous than the alternative, and so I told the judge that I'd rather go to prison.

The deputy DA ultimately got what they wanted when I chose prison over skid row. I could tell based on the look on my mom's face in the courtroom, that this wasn't the outcome she wanted, but I didn't care. At the time, I blamed her. I couldn't tell that she was trying to help me or that the deputy DA was trying to protect the public. I simply couldn't see how dangerous my addiction and mental health problems had become to me or the people around me.

# CHAPTER 9:
## Death Spiral

*"The hearts of people, moreover, are full of evil and there is madness in their hearts while they live, and afterward they join the dead."*
*(Ecclesiastes 9:3, NIV)*

I remember the day the California Department of Corrections and Rehabilitation (CDCR) came to pick up new prisoners. I was released from my holding area and taken down to the first floor of the jail near booking along with other prisoners. We were strip-searched, shackled, placed on the bus prisoners call the *Grey Goose*, and taken to Wasco State Prison. I was nervous about going to prison, but I was happy to see the sunshine again.

Wasco is a reception center for new prisoners, so housing is temporary for most, but the prison also has at least one area where people serve longer sentences. Sections or areas of prisons are referred to as yards. When we got off the bus at the prison, we were strip-searched again and put into holding cells. Any personal items that were in your possession upon arrest, are transported with you. If you have money on the books you get to send those possessions home. If you don't have money, the items must be donated to CDCR. I donated several items because I had no money.

After they ran me through processing, I was escorted to building 5 on B-yard. In 2002, this yard was general population level 3. In prison, yards have different levels. Based on your offense and prior criminal history, prisoners are assigned points. Points determine what level yard you will be on. Level 1 yards are for the lowest risk prisoners and level 4 yards are the highest risk. The higher the level yard, the more prison politics come into play and the more dangerous the yard. I knew nothing about prison or its politics. There were rules for everything and stepping out of line could get you in a wreck with your racial group or gang.

When I walked into the pod, the first thing I noticed was the big sign on the wall that said, *No Warning Shots Will Be Fired.* If you think about it, it's ridiculous that people who may have only been sentenced to prison for drug possession got placed in an environment where violence could break out, or they could get shot.

As I walked to my cell, I noticed a small hole in my prison door (or the door next to mine) the size of a .223 caliber bullet. That is the caliber of the Mini-14 and AR-15 rifles guard's use. I also saw what looked like a chip in the concrete where the bullet may have ricocheted off the floor and hit the door.

Everyone stared at me through their door windows. Someone yelled, "Where are you from, wood?" Wood is short for peckerwood, a common name for white prisoners. I yelled back, "Fresno," and walked into my cell when the door opened. The cell was half the size of the cell in Fresno County. My cell-mate lay on his bunk and said nothing. About a week or two into my term, I asked him, "What are you in for." He said, "rape." I couldn't believe he said that to me. Even I knew no one in their right mind would ever admit they were incarcerated for rape on a general population yard.

His admission of rape put me in a bad position. The prison is supposed to place these types of inmates on special-needs yards along with snitches, gang dropouts, and guys that want protective custody because of a prison drug debt. They do this because, on general population yards these types of prisoners are green-lighted by other inmates. This means that there is an automatic green light to inflict violence on them, so they must be protected by prison staff. In fact, when you come onto a new yard someone from your own racial group or gang will come and ask to see your paperwork. They want to make sure you are not there for any unacceptable type of criminal offense.

I wrestled with what to do with this guy in my cell for a few days. The rules are simple when dealing with rapists in the general population; the solution is always violent. If the other white prisoners found out I had done nothing or even hesitated, I could find myself in trouble. In prison, racial groups and gangs deal with their own problems. In the general population, people of the same race or gang associate and are celled together. This means the rapist in my cell was a problem the white prisoners would have to deal with, but he was my cell-mate so the problem would ultimately fall to me to handle. I only had three or four months to do in prison. I didn't want to catch more time if I hurt this guy.

The white guy in the cell next to me was from Tarpey Village, where I grew up. He had been in and out of prison his whole adult life. I asked him on the down-low what to do, and he said, "He is your cellie (cell-mate); you have to handle it bro. If you don't, you get handled." It confirmed to me that if I didn't do anything and the other white guys found out, there would be violence against me.

It just so happened that on this day my cell-mate irritated me. I hit him while he was standing in front of the cell door, and he smacked his face on a 90-degree piece of angled concrete. It split his eye open. He started frantically banging on the door of the cell, trying to get the officer's attention. I hit him a few more times, and he started to fight back. The guy in the cell next to me cheered the whole thing on and the noise caught the attention of the other prisoners in the pod. They started cheering too.

Finally, the officers popped the door open, and cell extracted us. This means they forcefully dragged us out. They threw us on the floor and cuffed us both. I remember seeing this guy's blood on the floor. I thought, "Well, this will get me more time," but I was wrong.

On the way to the little holding cage where they put prisoners who cause problems, the officer asked me if I'd hit him because of his rape conviction. This gave me the impression that the guards had known all along. I don't think the guy was placed on that yard by accident. They released me back to my cell with no additional charges.

My next cell-mate was also from Tarpey Village. It was good to have some guys around me from where I grew up. It made my short stay much easier.

There were many violent incidences in the short amount of time I spent on that yard, including a fight between the southern Mexican and black inmates and other random white on white violence. Before I left, I was transferred from B yard to H yard. Unlike B yard, H yard is open dorms and not cells but there was violence there as well. From H yard, I was transferred to A yard before going home. When I was on A yard, I met a guy from Kern County who is well known in prison. He said he had been in and out of prison his whole life. He told me, "Try and do something different with yourself. Prison is no kind of life." I agreed with him. I never wanted to go back.

When I was paroled, I moved back in with my parents, but I didn't feel welcomed there. My new parole officer was a female. She was a tiny redhead with a Texas accent. She looked like a redheaded pixie with handcuffs, but this lady was no joke. I had no doubt that she would send me back to prison if I stepped out of line. I was designated high control by parole because of the nature of my case and my mental health issues. High control is a designation usually reserved for violent offenders and gang members.

It wasn't long before I started using drugs again. Because I took medication in prison, I was enrolled in the Parole Outpatient Clinic (POC). POC handled psychiatric care for parolees. They made sure I saw a therapist and was prescribed medication. The craziest part of this relapse episode is that I am almost certain it began when POC began prescribing me abusable anxiety medication.

I briefly worked for my stepdad, but it didn't last. My son's grandmother gave me a car so I could get from place to place, but once again, I had been up for many days, was exhausted, lost control of the car and totaled it.

I remember getting out of the car and deciding I needed to run from the scene. I didn't want to talk to the police. When you're on parole, you can't have police contact. I ran away but then decided to walk back and face the music. I took my parole ID and shoved it into the dirt before the police came, hoping they wouldn't figure out I was on parole.

When the police got there, they placed me in the back of the cruiser and a male officer shined a light in my eyes, asking me if I was under the influence. I said no. The female officer in the front looked up my name and determined I was on high-control parole.

I should have been arrested on the spot for suspicion of being under the influence and for police contact. The female officer told me they were contacting my parole officer but after a few minutes, they released me, called my mom, and let her pick me up from the scene. The next week when I went to the parole office to drug test, I thought I would be arrested and taken in but when I apologized for the accident she asked, "What accident?" Shortly after this incident, my parole officer's supervisor took over my case.

I had tested positive several times for meth and opioids, and parole put me through several residential treatment programs. At some point during my ongoing meth use, my body became hyper-sensitive to meth. If I even took a little, I became psychotic. I continued to drink alcohol and take other drugs.

When I finished the last parole-ordered program, I transferred to a sober living facility in downtown Fresno. It was a horrible place. It was overcrowded and loud.

Shortly after I moved into sober living, I ran into a childhood friend who had also been incarcerated. Our mothers had attended high school together and I'd known his mom most of my life. He said I should leave the sober living and stay with his mom.

While I was living at his mom's, I relapse on alcohol and meth. Eventually, I wasn't welcome at my friend's mom's house, and I could no longer go back to my mom's.

Somehow, I had run into some family members that I had not seen in a while. They were God-fearing people. They had loved my biological dad and didn't want to see me follow in his footsteps. They let me sleep on the couch, put me to work in their business, and took me to church.

I continued to take pills, drink, and see various women. Eventually, they determined they were wasting their time and asked me to leave. I went back into sober living, which my mother helped pay for, but I wasn't sober.

The house manager sold oxycodone right out of the house. I bought oxycodone from him, was drinking and using meth, but when my addiction began to cause trouble in the house, he kicked me out. I had no choice but to go back to my parents.

My mental health had really deteriorated at this point. I was so psychotic from the meth use that I self-admitted to hospitals several times that year. It's hard to explain how dark my life felt. I was convinced I was going to die just like my dad. I prayed all the time and begged God to help me, but I felt beyond His reach. The only reason I didn't kill myself was that I didn't want to put my son through what I went through with the loss of my dad. I also knew I would have to face God if I dropped the hammer on myself. I wasn't prepared to face consequences of that magnitude.

Even at my very worst, I hoped God would intervene. I kept asking myself how I survived all the car accidents without a scratch if God didn't have a plan for my life. How did I survive the overdoses? Why would God reveal himself to me at different times in my life and constantly send spiritual people across my path only to have me waste away and die? Why did so many people randomly tell me He had a plan for me if it wasn't true, and where was He in all of this?

In the midst of all of my confusion and misery, God showed up once again. My mom, who was always trying to get me to church, actually got me there one night. It was a special service on a Friday night, and I was high on heroin. I sat down and listened to this woman give the most bizarre message. It was about a character in the Bible who had a prideful heart. God struck him with insanity because he refused to give glory to God or acknowledge the sovereignty of God in his life. I remembered my mom reading me this story when I was little. God struck him with madness for a time to humble him but restored him in the end. I thought to myself, "I am not glorifying God either or acknowledging his sovereignty over my life. I wondered if God was allowing me to suffer to get my attention?" I was certainly crazy.

My mom dragged me up to the altar for prayer. A lady who I had never met, approached me and told me God wanted to tell me something. She then proceeded to speak to me as if on God's behalf: "I have called you from the time you were a little boy, and you know it. I will restore you; I will give you your heart's desire; only come aside with me for a while, my beloved son." There I was standing in the same church, at the same altar, in the same spot where I had first encountered the Lord more than twenty years before at the age of 8, hearing once again that God had a plan for me.

I left with a bit of hope, but for months, I continued to use drugs and drink, bouncing around from place to place.

I kept finding people that liked to take in strays. I stayed with one woman I met at a recovery program some years back, and it was a stable environment, but I was still using and drinking, and my mental health issues were horrible.

One morning, I had been up all night on meth and didn't come home. I wandered around Fresno exhausted, psychotic, and hearing voices. I headed down Shaw Avenue in the late morning and came to the 41-freeway overpass. I decided that I was done with life, and I was going to jump. I kept staring at the traffic movement because I wanted to time it right. I was so sad my life had ended up this way. I wasn't more than a mile away from where my father had been shot and killed. I remember taking a piece of paper and pencil out of the backpack I had, and I wrote my son a note to tell him I loved him and that none of this was his fault.

While I was writing the note, I was flooded with sorrow. I remember a question that came to my mind suddenly, "Can't you endure this pain a little longer, for your son's sake?" I believe that thought came from God because my son is all I cared about and the only thing that would have deterred me from jumping that day. I tore up the note, feeling so ashamed, and walked past the freeway. I was millimeters from suicide that day.

Due to my continued drug use, I could no longer remain with the woman I had been staying with, so I moved in with a couple who were supposedly in recovery. I came to discover they were very addicted to opioids. Needless to say, my opioid addiction escalated while I was there. I had to leave there as well because I couldn't pay rent.

I had begun seeing a new girl shortly before I almost attempted suicide. I moved in with her and her mom. My girlfriend's mother was in recovery, but my girlfriend and I were both using drugs.

Eventually, her mom kicked me out and my girlfriend came with me. At this point, this girl and I were living out of a car.

I had managed to get a job with one of my stepdad's subcontractors doing electrical work. We slept in my parent's work parking lot in the car so I could wake up and walk down the street to work.

I didn't perform well on the job. Some days I left early because I couldn't function. Eventually, I was fired from the company.

This pushed me over the edge. I had lost all support, was severely addicted, suicidally depressed, homeless, on parole, and jobless. I failed at being a good father, had been married and divorced twice, and couldn't stay employed. Addiction programs didn't help me stay clean for long, and the medication wasn't working. I had hit rock bottom. I couldn't take it anymore.

I decided to go and visit my first wife's mother, who had been a support to me through all this mess, but I had a plan. I knew they owned guns. They were in a locked garage cabinet. I went into the garage while they were busy, unscrewed the cabinet hinges, and took one of the firearms. I told myself it was for my protection since I was homeless, but I also was seriously thinking about using it on myself.

My former father-in-law saw me take the gun and hide it. My former mother-in-law called my mom and told her I was incoherent and armed. My mom says she pulled over and prayed and then called Clovis PD to tell them the situation. She begged the dispatcher to tell the officers not to kill me. My ex-mother-in-law had managed to get me into the house. She asked me what I wanted the gun for and who did I plan to use it on, and I said, "Me." She burst into tears but got me to sit on the couch.

When the officers arrived, they came into the house with guns drawn, but I vaguely recall her sitting on my lap. I guess she figured they wouldn't shoot if she was in their way. They made her get up, and then they cuffed and searched me. They found ammunition in my pocket. Instead of taking me directly to jail, they called an ambulance to take me to the psychiatric unit, where I was admitted.

After I sobered up a little, I began looking for ways to escape from the hospital. I didn't want to go back to prison. I went into one of the rooms where they had these reclining bed-like chairs and looked up at the ceiling. There were some broken tiles. I stood on the chair and punched the ceiling and broke one of the tiles. A county guard came into the room and asked me if I had heard anything. I shook my head and he left

A few minutes later, I broke out another tile, and this time when he came in, I had tiles in my hand and maneuvered as if I was going the throw them at him. I don't recall how the staff got me into a locked safe room, but I think they may have given me sedatives. All I remember was being yanked up out of my bed by my parole officer and another officer and escorted to their car in my hospital gown. They took me to Fresno County Jail. I was there for four days before I was again placed back on the bus and taken back to prison.

# CHAPTER 10:

## Out of the Darkness and Into the Light

*"My son, don't despise the Lord's discipline, and don't despise*
*his rebuke, because the Lord disciplines those he loves,*
*as a father the son he delights in." (Proverbs 3:11-12, NIV)*

The first time I went to prison, I was on a level 3 yard. Although I wasn't in for long, it was long enough to learn about the politics and violence which happens in prison on higher-level yards. I dreaded going back. For months before I was arrested, I had dreams about returning to prison. I wasn't well and felt too vulnerable to go back inside. I was sick mentally and emotionally; I was out of shape and was really out of hope. Yet, I found myself on the bus back to prison for a parole violation.

This time they put me on a level 2 yard where the prison politics were minimal. I was locked up in Wasco reception with people I knew, so I felt more comfortable. I was so burned out from the drugs and damage I had done to my body that I couldn't think clearly and felt a crushing sorrow in my soul.

It felt like darkness had closed in on me and permeated every fiber of my being. I hated being awake, but my sleep was restless and filled with nightmares. My life was so dark, that even the backdrop of my dreams reflected that reality. If I was in a building in my dream, it was dark. If I was outside, it was night. It was as if my subconscious mind had no conception of light. I saw no light in the world when I was awake either. It was deeper than depression; it was despair.

About a week after I arrived, I was called to appear before what I think was the Board of Prison Hearings (BPH). I had no idea what this was because I didn't have to see them the first time I went to prison. My court-appointed attorney pulled me into the room and told me that state parole recommended an evaluation for alternative sentencing. As I understood the attorney, I would be evaluated and possibly placed in a state psychiatric hospital. He told me flat out that I didn't want that. The Board of Prison Hearings received the following recommendation from Parole

> "*Michael Prichard is a 30-year-old first termer, having been committed to CDCR for a probation violation, stemming from the conviction of PC245a. It is noted that the probation violation involved his failure to attend and complete drug treatment, as well as the abuse of psychotropic medications. Since releasing to parole supervision on 8/30/04, he has suffered two violations for the Use of Methamphetamine, as well as the Use of Codeine....*
>
> *It should be noted that throughout the period of Parole, Prichard has been exposed to a sundry of treatment modalities, including residential drug treatment programs, outpatient treatment programs, individual private therapy, placement on psychotropic medications and POC....*
>
> *The AOR has concerns over the mental health issues of Prichard and his family history of suicide. The current episode of depression and violations of Parole, as well as suicidal thoughts, are evidence of his erratic behavior. His family and ex-wife feel that long-term survival can only be achieved through long-term psychiatric intervention. Due to the nature of the circumstances surrounding Prichard's behavior, the AOR has no other recommendation but to refer him to the BPH for the appropriate disposition in this matter.*"

*Michael Prichard M.S.*

*(RSTS Case Status Report, March 28, 2006)*

Some of the information included in the report above was inaccurate but, regardless, it painted a bleak picture. The attorney at my hearing advocated for me to the Board of Prison Hearings, and they gave me an eight-month prison violation instead. When I returned to my pod, I walked around aimlessly. Another prisoner handed me a tract about prayer. It seemed so random. Did I look that desperate? I was desperate. Two things kept me from suicide up to that point; I didn't want my son to experience the pain I felt in losing my dad, and I was terrified to face God in my condition.

I remember laying on my bunk, reading this prayer tract with tears streaming down my face. It touched my heart. I didn't care if other prisoners surrounded me. I don't even think anyone noticed. I whispered a prayer to God. I just told Him I was ready to surrender and asked for His help. I recall telling God that He would have to make the change because I couldn't.

The difference in this prayer from all my others is that it was devoid of an agenda. I wasn't asking God to get me out of trouble; it was a prayer of surrender. I just gave up and looked to God to see what He would do if anything.

I felt the hand of God on the whole situation I was in, but I had little faith that a man as broken as me could be fixed. I knew God had a plan for my life at one point, but I had run from it. It felt like I was checkmated in the game of life by God himself. I knew God was dealing with me, but I also wasn't sure of God's intentions toward me. I had often viewed God as a God of wrath and anger. I also had so much guilt over the life I had lived and the people I had hurt that I couldn't imagine that God's intentions toward me were good, but I hoped they were.

In the weeks after the prayer, my mind cleared, and I began to have hope. Hope slowly replaced suicidal ideation. The hope didn't come from me. I felt something inside me changing that I couldn't explain.

About eight weeks into my prison violation, I received a letter from my mom. It was heartbreaking. She told me that she could no longer have contact with me. I felt abandoned by the one person I never thought would leave me. I could tell she meant it. I was so sad. Alone.

I later found out from my mom that during that time, God had spoken to her heart, telling her to take her hands off me. She said God impressed upon her that even though I came through her, I didn't belong to her; I belonged to Him. It crushed my mom to have to let go but she had to.

It wasn't just my mom, everyone in my life was done with me. Looking back, I see that God was working to sever the strands of toxic co-dependent relationships. Now, all I had was God, and He was going to do something that only He could do. He was going to fix Michael. But first He isolated me away from everything I knew. The church lady I mentioned earlier in the story, who spoke over me claiming she had a message from God, had said that God would restore me and give me the desires of my heart. Still, I would have to come away with God for a while. I didn't know what she meant at the time, and I had doubts that what she said was even from God, but it was going to become clear to me soon. If I was in prison by God's will, coming away with God wasn't a suggestion, it was a divine summons.

I felt a little relieved I would no longer have ties to my family because I wouldn't have to deal with their disappointment in me, but to be honest, I knew I'd see my mom again eventually. I missed my son tremendously though, and I wanted contact with him. I desired for him to see me in a healthy state again and it gave me the incentive to get healthy. Still, prison is dangerous and often the worst place for recovery. I didn't know how I was going to get well in that place.

About a month before I left Wasco State Prison to mainline prison, I began to read the Bible a little here and there. To be honest, I knew what it contained because I was raised in the church. I wasn't ready to hear the full weight of what God had to say just yet, but God was working in me already. Even though this new attitude was forming in me, I had still been drinking periodically in Wasco. Some of the other guys made *pruno* or jailhouse wine. I decided to stop and took my last drink on May 24, 2006. I also had this crazy thought that I should taper off the medication CDCR was giving me. I just had a sense that I would not need them anymore.

Abruptly stopping medication is common for people with mental health issues, and I had done it before with disastrous results, so I didn't trust my mind completely. The feeling I had about going off my medication was different this time. I began to feel inexplicably hopeful. You have to remember that the only decent period of sobriety I ever had, I only accomplished because I was on medication. The doctors had convinced my family and me that lifelong medication was mandatory for my wellbeing and that I'd never be able to not take them and remain well.

In fact, a few years before this prison violation, my aunt paid thousands to have me evaluated at a place called the Amen Clinic, trying to get to the bottom of all my mental health issues. The Amen clinics use highly advanced computer brain imaging to look at overall brain functioning and assess brain damage. They use the brain images coupled with the patient's medical and psychiatric history to inform treatment. The Amen brain scans and tests detected visible brain damage from exposure to drugs and possibly other injuries. My long-standing persistent psychiatric symptoms, coupled with the brain scans, led the doctors to conclude that I had damage resulting in dysfunction in the following areas of my brain:

- Pre-Frontal Cortex
- Left Temporal Lobe
- Deep Limbic System
- Basal Ganglia

Some of the symptoms associated with these findings include extreme anxiety, depression, mood irritability, aggression, dark and violent thoughts, hyperactivity, impulsivity, distractibility, lack of empathy, decreased motivation, and sleep problems.

I'd suffered from all of those in the extreme for decades. The Amen Clinic's findings matched all the prior diagnoses: bipolar II with anxious features, ADHD, and substance use disorder.

I didn't respond to any form of treatment for long, so I didn't receive a favorable prognosis from most doctors. It isn't hard to understand why parole thought I should be evaluated for alternative psychiatric treatment. But medication didn't fix the problem; it only stabilized me enough to get by day to day and getting by isn't living.

I didn't thrive on the medication. It had side effects, and I hated them. I was nervous about going off, but I figured if I was going to lose my mind, it was better to do it in a controlled environment. I tapered off slowly with no ill effects after a month. I felt sharper off the medication, more alert. By the time I received news that I would be sent to Soledad State Prison, I had tapered off most of the medication.

On the bus ride to Soledad State Prison, I felt a little nervous but also oddly excited, almost how I'd feel on a field trip when I was in school. Maybe it was because I was feeling healthier and hopeful. Soledad is a historical prison but also a training facility for CDCR officers.

The prisoners on the bus all entered the reception area of the prison for processing, but I was the only one to be given a cell that day. Officers placed the rest in overflow gyms. The prisons were running out of room for prisoners because of antiquated efforts to deal with drug offenders.

After I left processing, I walked down this long declining hallway with colorful murals painted on the walls. Off the hallway, there were various wings where prisoners were housed. The officers escorted me to the C wing of Soledad's central yard.

As I entered the wing, I passed a guard's station to the left and then entered a concrete open area with metal tables. To the right and the left were lines of cells on the floor with stairways leading to second and third tiers of cells. The dayroom was full of people when I walked in, holding my box of stuff. People stopped to stare. I watched some guys ironing their clothes and remember wondering where they thought they were going that they needed their clothes to be ironed.

I was placed on the bottom floor in a cell with an old lifer who was convicted of murdering his wife. Someone told me that the central yard (my yard) was made up mostly of lifers because a controlled level 2—a level 2 yard with cells rather than open dorms—was as low as a lifer could go in CDCR.

My prison cell was six feet wide by nine feet long. The paint was peeling on the ceiling, and peanut butter, which my cell-mate used to try to attract birds, coated the metal grating on the windows. The old man was polite and kind. I had nothing, and he used to share his tea with me, which I appreciated.

A day or two after I arrived, some huge white guy came to my cell and asked to see my paperwork. I remember looking at this guy and wondering who he killed to get there. He told me the rules and warned me to stay away from drugs. Drugs were everywhere. Heroin and meth were common.

During my stay, someone in the cell across from me overdosed on heroin and died. The guards pulled him and his mattress into the middle of the dayroom. He was on his back in his boxers and wasn't breathing. The officers just left him there. It must have been a full 30 minutes before any medical staff came to him. It looked like they put portable shock paddles on his chest to try to revive him. But to me, it looked like they were just going through the motions to say they followed protocol. The dude had been dead for a while. This is one of the many ugly events I witnessed in prison.

I had to remain in my cell for my first ten days before staff allowed me to go out to the yard. It's part of the classification process. During those ten days, I tapered off my remaining medication.

When I cleared classification, I could go out into the yard. I walked down the large hallway, cleared the metal detector, and joyfully walked into the sunlight.

Soledad Central had a huge yard area with a massive track, and pull-up and dip bars. The prison was close to the coast, so it was never hot. The yard was segregated by race, so I had to learn where to go and where not to. Mostly, in the beginning, I just walked the track.

There was sporadic violence on the yard. One guy got his neck cut open almost right in front of me. I think he was medevacked to a local hospital. I heard he survived. Violence and traumatic events are prevalent in prison.

Inside my wing, some cell changes happened right after I arrived. An inmate who had been in my wing for a long time told me this wasn't the norm. It didn't feel coincidental. It felt like God was doing things to help me. A few of the people who were moved into my wing befriended me and even served as short-term spiritual mentors during my time there.

I wrote letters to my mom, only asking for prayer. I wrote my former mother-in-law and asked for a Bible. My mom sent me *Purpose Driven Life* by Rick Warren.

Even though she wouldn't talk to me, I knew she'd continue to pray for me. When the Bible came, I decided I would do two things daily: exercise on the yard and spiritual devotion.

I first began reading *The Purpose Driven Life*. I read the book as instructed every morning for 40 days and prayed while my cellmate was out. This book provided me with a special kind of hope and some direction. I began reading my Bible as well but had no guidance on where to start.

A Christian guy who befriended me gave me a printed schedule to read the Bible in a year. I cut it in half and taped half in the front of my Bible and half in the back. I enjoyed reading the Bible. I had always been fascinated by God even though I was scared of Him. Growing up, I had a fear and a love for God at different times. I had encounters with the Spirit of God, and I was told over and over that God had a plan and purpose for my life. I just didn't know what people meant when they said it.

In prison, I only had four things to worry about: eating, sleeping, working out, and reading. The one thing prison did for me was to shield me from the stress of the outside world long enough to get healthy, but I had to keep my head down and stay focused.

Prison does not have a positive effect on most people. Prison generally doesn't make people better. It can be traumatizing and being a convict with a record is a considerable barrier to life success when people get out. I tell people I recovered in prison despite it, not because of it. I felt that this was my last chance to try and pull it together, and I pursued it.

I finally knew I didn't have the power to change on my own. I couldn't just shrug off trauma, lifelong mental health problems, addiction, and all the accumulated guilt and shame keeping me tethered to the cycle of behavior that was slowly killing me. Therapy, medication, and rehabs had little lasting impact on me, and these were the best solutions society had to offer. If change was going to happen in my case, it was going to come from a spiritual source. The root of my most significant issues was spiritual anyway, though I had always attributed the problem to other things.

I began working out on the yard. This helped my mind heal and my body get strong. The only time I exercised in the past was when I was wrestling. It was hard to begin working out regularly, but it made my anxiety decrease and helped me sleep. I also began to go to every chapel service offered.

God saw to it that I had everything I needed to grow spiritually inside the prison walls. It's incredibly difficult to describe what it was that transitioned inside me, what exactly allowed me to suddenly be hopeful, enthusiastic about change, and disciplined enough to take steps toward change. But I know the change began right after I prayed and surrendered to God, and it continued as I read the Bible and other Christian books.

I cannot look back and point to a date on the calendar and say, God healed me on that day, or I went to the chapel one Sunday, was prayed for, and then I was all better. It didn't happen like that at all. God was restructuring my whole worldview through scripture and books. The Spirit of God was also bringing to my mind all the experiences I had with Him throughout my life, and it all began to weave together and make sense.

As I began to read, the Spirit of God began to open my eyes to the text, and I saw how my life fit into a grand plan. It's hard to explain, but I literally felt the presence of God with me in my cell on some days. I read the scriptures with clarity. I was raised in the church, so I knew the Bible, but suddenly, I connected the dots in the Bible as if my IQ had jumped 20 points.

It wasn't just intellectual understanding, it penetrated me. I couldn't stop reading. I needed to hear from God, and I pressed in with vigor. I was hungry for it. I read in the morning, worked out in the afternoon, and read in the evening until bedtime. I read dozens of chapters per day. Months into this process, I'd wake up praying and praising God in that twilight state when I was half asleep and half awake. I no longer had bad dreams, just peaceful sleep.

As I read the Bible, I was in awe of the magnitude and power of the God it described, and this power was at work, healing me in a prison cell in California, thousands of years after the words were written. Even though the scriptures were healing, the process wasn't always comfortable. At times it was excruciating. I would feel comfort from verses I read in the text, but the scriptures also cut me deep. In chapter 4, verses 12-13 of the book of Hebrews in the Bible, it says:

*"For the word of God is alive and active. Sharper than any double-edged sword, it penetrates even to dividing soul and spirit, joints and marrow; it judges the thoughts and attitudes of the heart. Nothing in all creation is hidden from his sight. Everything is uncovered and laid bare before the eyes of him to whom we must give an account."* (NIV)

That is what scripture did; it judged me. It didn't judge me like a person would judge another person. People are flawed and hypocritical and have no right to judge in a way that condemns others. The scriptures judged me from the point of righteous perfection, and it does have the power to convict and condemn. I looked in the mirror of scripture and saw the perfection of God against my imperfection.

Considering who I had been, the reality of who God is hit me like a wrecking ball. You might be asking, how is getting hit by a spiritual wrecking ball in any way healing? Well, it smashed through the angry, resentful, rebellious attitudes of my heart. Here is the truth: because of the trauma that I experienced early in life and because of the mental health and addiction issues, I saw myself as a victim, and the helping professionals in my life had co-signed and even helped instill this narrative in me. To explain my behavior, doctors told me I had a chemical imbalance. Therapists told me that I was a good person that bad things happened to, and that I wasn't at fault for my issues.

That never entirely sat right with me because despite the legitimate trauma I had experienced that influenced my choices early on and the mood disorder I struggled with, I knew that my heart was corrupt, and my character had become increasingly rotten at the core. As hard as I tried, I couldn't embrace explanations about my behavior that completely removed my accountability and attributed it to something else.

The people who tried to convince me that I was a good person who had just been through some hard things, had no right to tell me that. They didn't know me. But I knew me, and I knew I was guilty of so many things that had involved conscious choice, even if painful life events beyond my control influenced those choices. I couldn't assign blame to everything else as if I were somehow absent from the equation.

Embracing the victim mentality for so many years had negative effects on my psyche. It made me angry at God and people. It made me feel entitled. I figured since I had been dealt a bad hand in life, the world owed me something. When I didn't get what I felt I should get, it led to self-pity and hopelessness. It made mental health issues far worse. It drove me deeper into my addiction and made it impossible to resolve the guilt and shame I felt over things I had done to myself and others.

Seeing myself as a victim also didn't help resolve the fear that I'd have to stand before God someday and give an account of my life. The anger and resentment I had toward God and others, as well as the unresolved guilt and shame over wrongs that I had committed against God and others are what made me sick mentally, emotionally, physically, and relationally.

As I read the Bible, my sad condition became more apparent as God showed me who He is and who I was apart from His grace and mercy. Like all people, I was capable of doing some good things some of the time but none of those good things met God's standard of good and no amount of human good that I could do would ever be able to erase my past sins. I had become the worst version of myself, and I knew that I was in so much trouble spiritually because my own conscience relentlessly condemned me.

The Bible just confirmed what my conscience already told me about myself. It confronted me with the truth that I had refused to submit to, and I was suffering the consequences of many of my choices. I was a wounded person because of the blows that life dealt me but I was more wounded by the blows I dealt to myself.

I had been taught what was right and true but lived in opposition to those truths and suffered moral injury as a result. I had experienced God during periods of my life. I had always believed there was a plan and purpose for my life but always turned away. I was spiritually bankrupt.

I know that it may be hard for someone to understand how I can lay so much blame at my own feet considering the trauma and mental health struggles I experienced early on. It took me a long time to figure it out as well. It's undeniable that life beat me up in my early years. Trauma caused me pain and destabilized me emotionally.

Using substances young as a coping mechanism for emotional pain led to addiction, which ultimately took my life off course. My addiction brought out the worst in me and turned me into a lying, thieving, criminal, and a neglectful parent. Even if the pathway to becoming this horrible version of myself began with trauma that wasn't my fault, my conscience wouldn't let me off the hook for the part I played in allowing it to take me where it took me.

It's important to note that the seeds of the undesirable behaviors that manifested in my addiction were already present in me in childhood long before the substance use ever started, but a strong sense of right and wrong was present in me as well; I knew better. The pain and anger I experienced in my early years tilted me in the direction of wrongdoing. I couldn't always control my behavior, but I could sometimes, and when I didn't my conscience would let me know it. In fact, my drug use escalated faster and faster toward the end because I was trying to drown out the sound of my conscience constantly condemning my behavior even when I didn't feel entirely in control of it. Trauma only served as a contributing factor that helped steer me toward a path of self-destruction. I made decisions, impaired and immature as they were, that kept me on that path. I needed God to heal the pain caused by the trauma done to me because it was too deep for humans to reach, but I also needed healing in the form of forgiveness for the things I had done, and only God has the authority to offer true forgiveness. I needed to feel God's love because I couldn't love Him, myself, or anyone else without it. For all these reasons, human interventions alone could never be successful in my case. Humans cannot provide what only God has the power to give.

When I read the Bible, I knew it had not been explicitly written to me, but written for humanity. In communicating to people through the scripture, God shows us who He is and who we are. God is good and perfect, and we are morally flawed at our core. The Bible calls this moral corruption *sin*. Sin simply means *missing the mark*, like someone shooting a target and missing it. The Bible teaches that we all miss the mark because of this sin nature within,

*"…. for all have sinned and fall short of the glory of God."*
*(Romans 3:23, NIV)*

There are moral relativists that deny the concept of moral absolutes but trying to live out a relativistic philosophy in life isn't possible. Humans believe in right and wrong. If we didn't, we could never organize our lives and live together in societies. The Bible brings God's standards into focus and confirms what we already know to be true, and because of this, it's a glorious but terrifying book. It confronts us with the truth about our nature that we don't like to acknowledge and contains moral absolutes that infringe on our desire to live the way we choose without experiencing discomfort.

I avoided the Bible for years because I feared the God it described, but when I acknowledged its truth and applied the wisdom it provided to my life, God healed me and enabled me to use other tools I had learned in recovery up to that point. The Spirit of God working through the Bible was the spark that set the machine of change into motion in my life. That is the bottom line.

God uses different means to reach different kinds of people. God ultimately draws people by His love and grace, but grace takes on many forms. God draws some people with delicateness and gentleness and others with strong discipline. I was angry at God and ran from Him. I was angry, resentful, rebellious, refused to submit to authority, and felt justified in my behavior so God needed to correct my perspective and firmly establish His authority over my life in way that I could feel at the deepest level of my being. God knew what I had been through but He also knew the sinful attitudes of my heart and all the wrongs I had committed.

God's initial means of grace to me was strong correction. God still uses painful discipline and correction in my life at times because my heart is spring-loaded to rebel and go its own way if left to my own devices. To this day I still deviate from the good path at times and God in His mercy draws me back. I think this core tendency I have toward stubborn rebellion was evident to everyone but me.

Even my parole officer knew that my core issues were refusal to submit to authority and trusting my own faulty thinking. Shortly after I tested dirty for parole, the officer told me that I had never listened to anyone: not my parents, not my teachers, not law enforcement. He said I would have to submit to something higher than myself. He was right, but the authority I needed to submit to wasn't something, it was someone; the God who is. It had to be God because I didn't trust human authority, but I knew, or came to know, that God is trustworthy.

While I was in prison there were so many verses in the Bible God used to penetrate my hardened heart. The first Bible verses God used to correct and teach me are in Deuteronomy chapter 28, where God lays out blessings for obedience and curses for disobedience to the nation of Israel. Among the curses was this,

*"The Lord will afflict you with madness, blindness and confusion of mind. At midday you will grope about like a blind man in the dark. You will be unsuccessful in everything you do; day after day you will be oppressed and robbed, with no one to rescue you."*
*(Deuteronomy 28:28-29, NIV)*

This verse described my condition well. I thought, "Is it possible that I had lost my mind because I went my own way and refused to submit to God? Is everything I am going through linked to my own rebellious nature?" Then I read further:

*".... You will find no repose, no resting place for the sole of your foot. There the Lord will give you an anxious mind, eyes weary with longing, and a despairing heart. You will live in constant suspense, filled with dread both night and day, never sure of your life."*

*(Deuteronomy 28:65-66, NIV)*

This verse also described how I was feeling as a result of my choices. Refusing to submit to God's plan and going my own way destabilized my life. Then I read verses in the books of Jeremiah and Isaiah that cut me to the quick.

*"Have you not brought this on yourselves by forsaking the Lord your God when he led you in the way?" (Jeremiah 2:17, NIV)*

*"Your wickedness will punish you; your backsliding will rebuke you. Consider then and realize how evil and bitter it is for you when you forsake the Lord your God and have no awe of me, declares the Lord. The Lord Almighty." (Jeremiah 2:19, NIV)*

*"Your own conduct and actions have brought this upon you. This is your punishment; how bitter it is! How it pierces to the heart." (Jeremiah 4:18, NIV)*

*"I the Lord search the heart and examine the mind to reward a man according to his conduct, according to what his deeds deserve." (Jeremiah 17:10, NIV)*

*"I warned you when you felt secure, but you said I will not listen! This has been your way from your youth, you have not obeyed me." (Jeremiah 22:21, NIV)*

*"Is not my word like fire,' declares the Lord, 'and like a hammer that breaks a rock into pieces.'" (Jeremiah 23:29, NIV)*

*"You have forgotten God your Savior; you have not remembered
the Rock your Fortress." (Isaiah 17:10, NIV)*

*"This is what the Sovereign Lord, the Holy One of Israel says,
'In repentance and rest is your salvation, in quietness and trust is
your strength, but you would have none of it.'" (Isaiah 30:15, NIV)*

*"I am the Lord and there is no other; apart from me there is no god.
I will strengthen you, though you have not acknowledged me,
so that from the rising of the sun to the place of its setting
people may know there is none besides me. I am the Lord and
there is no other. I form the light and create darkness; I bring
prosperity and create disaster; I the Lord do all these things.....
Woe to him who quarrels with his maker." (Isaiah 45:5-7, & 9)*

These verses are only a select few with which God confronted
me. God had tried to reach me on many occasions throughout my
life, but I ran from his calling. My rebellion needed to be broken. I
knew that I was in prison, and my life was in shambles, at least in
part because of my choices and my refusal to answer that call. Being
confronted with the truth broke through my hardened heart. While
I was sitting in prison, the pain in my soul echoed the lament of the
prophet Jeremiah in the book of Lamentations after God dealt with
the rebellious behavior of his people by sending them into captivity.

The lamenting verses in the book lead to repentance and healing for me because I became convinced that I was also in captivity
so that God could correct my perspective and then grant me further
grace, just as He did with the people the book of Lamentations was
written to.

"My sins have been bound into a yoke;

by his hands they were woven together.

They have been hung on my neck,

and the Lord has sapped my strength.

He has given me into the hands

of those I cannot withstand." (Lamentations 1:14, NIV).

"This is why I weep

and my eyes overflow with tears.

No one is near to comfort me,

no one to restore my spirit." (Lamentations 1:16, NIV).

"The Lord is righteous,

yet I rebelled against his command." (Lamentations 1:18, NIV).

"See, Lord, how distressed I am!

I am in torment within,

and in my heart I am disturbed,

for I have been most rebellious." (Lamentations 1:20, NIV)

"My eyes fail from weeping,

I am in torment within;

my heart is poured out on the ground." (Lamentations 2:11, NIV)

"I am the man who has seen affliction

by the rod of the Lord's wrath.

He has driven me away and made me walk

in darkness rather than light;

indeed, he has turned his hand against me

again and again, all day long." (Lamentations 3:1-3, NIV)

"He has besieged me and surrounded me

with bitterness and hardship.

*He has made me dwell in darkness*

*like those long dead.*

*He has walled me in so I cannot escape;*

*he has weighed me down with chains." (Lamentations 3:5-7, NIV)*

*"He has barred my way with blocks of stone;*

*he has made my paths crooked." (Lamentations 3:9, NIV)*

*"I have been deprived of peace;*

*I have forgotten what prosperity is.*

*So I say, 'My splendor is gone*

*and all that I had hoped from the Lord.'*

*I remember my affliction and my wandering,*

*the bitterness and the gall.*

*I well remember them,*

*and my soul is downcast within me.*

*Yet this I call to mind*

*and therefore I have hope:*

*Because of the Lord's great love, we are not consumed,*

*for his compassions never fail.*

*They are new every morning;*

*great is your faithfulness.*

*I say to myself, 'The Lord is my portion;*

*therefore I will wait for him'*

*The Lord is good to those whose hope is in him,*

*to the one who seeks him;*

*it is good to wait quietly*

*for the salvation of the Lord.*

*It is good for a man to bear the yoke*

*while he is young.*

*Let him sit alone in silence,*

*for the Lord has laid it on him.*

*Let him bury his face in the dust—*

*there may yet be hope.*

*Let him offer his cheek to one who would strike him,*

*and let him be filled with disgrace.*

*For no one is cast off*

*by the Lord forever.*

*Though he brings grief, he will show compassion,*

*so great is his unfailing love.*

*For he does not willingly bring affliction*

*or grief to anyone.*

*To crush underfoot*

*all prisoners in the land,*

*to deny people their rights*

*before the Most High,*

*to deprive them of justice—*

*would not the Lord see such things?*

*Who can speak and have it happen*

*if the Lord has not decreed it?*

*Is it not from the mouth of the Most High*

*that both calamities and good things come?*

*Why should the living complain*

*when punished for their sins?*

*Let us examine our ways and test them,*

*and let us return to the Lord." (Lamentations 3:17-40, NIV)*

The Bible challenged the victim narrative I came to believe and told me the truth about who God was, who I was, and what needed to happen for me to change. That confrontation with truth brought sorrow but the kind of sorrow that led me away from my old life and toward God.

As I read scripture, the scripture confronted me. My emotions were raw, there was no alcohol or drugs to mask my pain, numb my anxious thoughts, or drown out my conscience. I often burst into tears when I was deeply convicted, and I asked for God's forgiveness. This happened daily for months, but I felt clean, washed, renewed, and forgiven in the end. All the weight lifted off me. I felt lighter, and the darkness disappeared. A moral structure began to form in me, and my conscience became even more sensitized.

In prison, after losing everything, I was happier than I had ever been. I was free even though I was in prison. It was the confrontation with God's holy, perfect, moral law that brought me to a place of repentance, but it was the grace that came through the gospel of Jesus Christ that provided, hope, and peace. I had been taught these truths growing up but never really understood them completely. The truth had always been there, but I couldn't perceive its value. After the correction from God's word had its effect, I began to key in on verses that highlighted God's peace and God's willingness to relate to humanity. Isaiah 55:7, Jeremiah 6:16, Jeremiah 33:3, and Ezekiel 18:30-31 were transformative verses for me:

*"Let the wicked forsake their ways and the unrighteous their thoughts.*
*Let them turn to the LORD, and he will have mercy on them,*
*and to our God, for he will freely pardon." (Isaiah 55:7, NIV)*

Pardon from God for my sinful behavior is what I needed most.

*"This is what the Lord says, 'Stand at the crossroads and look; ask for the ancient paths, ask where the good way is and walk in it and you will find rest for your soul.'" (Jeremiah 6:16 NIV)*

*"Call to me and I will answer you, and I will tell great and unsearchable things that you do not know." (Jeremiah 33:3, NIV)*

*"Repent! Turn away from all your offenses; then sin will not be your downfall. Rid yourselves of all the offenses you have committed, and get a new heart and a new spirit." (Ezekiel 18:30-31, NIV)*

I was at a crossroads in Soledad State Prison; Biblical teachings were the ancient paths, good way, and full of things I didn't know yet. If my soul was to remain at rest, I had to walk in God's direction, abandoning darkness and pursuing light. The ongoing abandonment of darkness and the pursuit of the light of love is the Christian life in a nutshell. To this day, the degree to which I pursue light and stay away from darkness, I find I either experience peace or distress.

During my time in prison, I read the Bible in sixty days; it consumed me. It was a massive shot of spiritual penicillin for a very sick soul. Even though I felt as though I had been taken to the woodshed by my heavenly father, when I left Soledad State Prison, I knew God loved me, was aware of me, had watched over me, and had a plan and purpose for me. That knowledge brought hope, and that hope was the light in the darkness of my soul. Knowing God was in control over everything brought peace. Darkness couldn't remain, and God's perfect love extinguished all my fear. The truth set me free, the word of God brought healing, and unlike human solutions, the healing was permanent.

# CHAPTER 11:

## Life in the Light

*"For I know the plans I have for you,' declares the Lord, "plans to prosper you and not to harm you, plans to give you a hope and future. Then you will call on me and come and pray to me, and I will listen to you. You will seek me and find me when you seek me with all your heart. I will be found by you,' declares the Lord, 'and will bring you back from captivity." (Jeremiah 29:11-14, NIV)*

I was paroled on November 12, 2006, in the early morning. I was full of hope mixed with uncertainty. Even though she was no longer talking to me, my mother sent me dress-out clothes to leave the prison. The gesture surprised me.

When I walked out of the gates of Soledad State Prison, I knew I had a new lease on life. I felt the presence of God within me and around me. That day all the paroled prisoners piled into the van, and the correctional officer took us to the bus station and made us buy bus tickets to take us to our respective home cities.

On the bus ride back to Fresno, I looked out the window at all the coastal trees, thinking how beautiful they were. Nothing had been beautiful in the world before. Everything seemed brighter, more real. It felt like I had awoken from a long coma. I was renewed. Deep gratitude filled my heart.

The day before I left prison, I kneeled at my bunk and prayed. I thanked God for what He had done for me and asked Him to show the world what He could do with someone who surrendered to His will and turned his life over to His control. He continues to answer that prayer.

Since the main reason I wrote this book is to place God's attributes on display and give hope, I will briefly tell you what God has done since that morning.

I arrived in Fresno that evening. I took some of the $200.00 gate money from CDCR to get a hotel. I didn't have an ID, and some shady hotel clerk tried to trick me out of the money. I considered walking the streets all night and reporting to parole in the morning.

Instead, I called my former mother-in-law to see if she could help. As always, and true to her nature, she picked me up and took me to dinner. We talked for quite a while. She gave me some encouragement and booked me a nice hotel room next to the parole office.

It's hard to explain how strange it felt to be back in Fresno after being completely transformed. Everything was the same, yet I saw it through different eyes. I wasn't who I had been when I last walked the same streets.

Before I left Fresno, I was on death's door. My mother had been planning my funeral. Now, I had a sound, sober clear-thinking mind. Less than a year earlier, my life was a curse on my family and community, but now I had hope. Although I didn't know it at the time, God was going to use my experiences to make me a significant community asset.

The following day, I showed up bright and early at the parole office. I didn't know if I'd have the same officer I had before I went to prison or a new one. They assigned me a new officer. Although I didn't expect kindness from parole, this man seemed hostile.

Because I had been paroled homeless, I had no address. Parole likes to keep track of parolees. The officer insisted that I go to the Fresno Rescue Mission, but I refused, which irritated him even more. I was hoping to transfer out of Fresno to a program in San Francisco.

My ex-wife had taken my son to live there so she could complete a Ph.D. program. The officer dashed those plans. I told him I was willing to go to a local parolee re-entry program because at least there I'd get to look for a job and get on with my life. He agreed and took me there immediately.

On the way there, I told him what happened to me in prison. He didn't seem to buy it, though he did soften up a little and give me some encouragement in the parking lot.

The parolee re-entry program was referred to as an addiction treatment program, but there was little treatment conducted there. I did not receive one counseling session. It was an old motel about a mile south of what could be considered Fresno's skid row. Barbed wire surrounded the grounds like a prison.

I could sleep there at night, but I'd have to leave during the day to look for work. My counselor at the program told me that if I didn't have a job in 30 days, I would be out. They would keep most of the money I earned until I left, retaining 25% to pay for room and board. It felt like I left one prison only to enter another, but I was determined to make it and I had God with me.

I shared a single hotel room with three roommates. A few of them appeared to have significant mental health and behavioral problems. It was rough. I called my ex-mother-in-law and asked for a bus pass. Once again, true to her nature, she obliged and also brought me a brand-new mountain bike from her brother, who had also tried to help me at various points in my life. My family had been removed from my life, but God provided other people to help.

I was a stereotypical parolee with a backpack and a mountain bike, riding around looking for work. I needed a valid I.D. On the first day out of the program, I went to the Social Security Office to get a copy of my social security card. On day two, I bicycled to the DMV to get a new copy of my license. On day three, I went to an employment agency to get a listing of jobs and to create a resume. Luckily, I did have some work experience to put on my resume. I then visited second-hand closets to see what clothes they could give me and used my gate money to buy some very cheap clothes for interviewing and daily wear.

For the next two and a half weeks, I bicycled from place to place, turning in my resume. Another employment agency helped me fax my resume to various employers. When I had five days left to find employment, a local glass installation company contacted me for an interview.

I walked into the interview with a level of peace and confidence that I knew was from God. Because of my construction experience and the fact that I had a valid license, they gave me a shot as a glass installer. It paid very little, but it allowed me to stay in the program for six months and save money.

The company was on the other side of town. This required that I wake up at 4:00 am in the dead of a very cold Fresno winter. I scarfed down a quick breakfast and biked to downtown Fresno where I could catch a specific bus to take me to the other side of town. Then, I continued to bike to my job.

Because I was on probation for my job, they told me that if I was late once, they would let me go. This process continued for over five months. Work was exhausting, and the process to get to work was exhausting and nerve-racking, but God was with me in various ways. Twice during my work probationary period, I arrived in downtown Fresno and the morning bus didn't show up. I remember praying, "God, please help, you know my situation," as I waited for the next bus.

If that next bus had followed their whole route, I would've arrived to work late and would have been let go. However, on both those days, two different drivers took the bus off course and dropped me off directly in front of my work so I wouldn't be late.

Another example of God's care happened while I was out on the job. I finished installing glass at a lady's house, and as I was leaving, she told me she had a box of clothes her son left behind when he went to college. As I was his size, she gave me the clothes. It touched me that she was willing to give me, a stranger, these clothes. I would have been happy with anything, but when I opened the box, they were all high-end brand-named items. I knew it wasn't just the kindness of this stranger, but God knew what I needed, and He was taking care of me. This instance and dozens like it came at the right time to meet a specific need in response to my prayers.

My counselor at the re-entry program had also sponsored someone who used to come into the program to tell his story. He had gone through the re-entry program himself and was doing pretty well for himself. I needed a guide and asked him to work with me. He decided to be my sponsor.

Outside of work, I attended a local church downtown, but I wasn't connecting there. I have always had a difficult time connecting in conventional church settings. My new sponsor picked me up from the program and took me to a small church he attended full of convicts and people in recovery. I was home. I became very involved in that church and attended Bible studies and served the community on Saturdays.

My sponsor pushed me to leave the program after six months. I used the money I saved to buy a little car and went into a sober living house. Shortly after, I began mentoring men at the Fresno Rescue Mission who would come to the church I attended. I was early in recovery, but I was on fire for God and needed to give back what I had been given. This church seemed like a magical place for people in recovery. I really needed it, but it was also very unhealthy in ways I couldn't see initially.

When I left the program and entered sober living, I had been clean and sober for 14 months. My mom heard from others that I was doing well, so she allowed me to come around on special occasions. I had also been seeing my son periodically. Eventually, I rented a house with a friend from church. It was great. We had church BBQs there and lots of good fellowship, but I was lonely.

I got up very early in the morning, prayed, read my Bible, went to work, came home, attended a church event or a recovery meeting in the evening, and went to bed. I had to keep my life regimented for my own safety, but I really wanted a partner in my life. I wanted to be married. I wanted someone I could share my life with and prayed for it constantly. I wanted a woman who loved God, and who was in recovery herself. I truly believed that I would not be able to relate to a woman who had not walked a path similar to my own.

Since my past relationships were all failures, I decided to pray and wait for God to pick someone for me. When I was praying, I'd say to God. "I believe you have a woman for me. I don't know who she is or what she is doing but if she is still in her addiction, please clean her up and bring her to me."

God had a timing. I had been going to church with the woman (Darlene) I would marry the whole time. She had been clean and sober a year longer than me. God cleaned me up and brought me to her. My last full day in prison had been her birthday. It was strange. I recall that she began talking to me periodically during church events. We just hit it off.

I wanted to get to know her better, so I invited her and her daughter to a BBQ. I tried to sit next to her, but she didn't seem to realize I was interested in her. When one of the women at the church told her I was interested, she didn't believe her. She did invite me to see a movie that afternoon with her and her daughter.

I left the BBQ and went with her, and we have not left each other's side since. We did everything together and still do. She was and is my best friend. We married eight months later. My family loved her, but only her oldest daughter supported our marriage, so it wasn't without struggles.

Her family thought she was rushing into another relationship with another unstable guy, which was her pattern in her addiction. I may have looked like one of the others, but God had transformed my life and hers.

She tells me now that she hadn't been looking for a husband but that my prayers to God must have won out. Before she got clean and became a Christian, she had tried to make it work with other men and had bad luck. There was abuse in her last relationship, and I think she had given up. I believe God chose us for each other and worked with us separately to bring us together later.

Eventually, my mom let me move into my grandfather's vacant home to live rent-free while rebuilding my life. After Darlene and I married, she moved in and we lived in that house for about two years. We fixed it up and hoped to buy it, but it wasn't in the cards. Darlene managed hair salons, and I worked as a glass installer, but I wanted to go into ministry. I went back to school while I worked.

I had no computer skills. In the beginning, I'd hand-write papers and Darlene would type them. I didn't know what I was doing, but I had a passion for God, and I knew there was more for us than what we were doing in early recovery.

Slowly things began to crumble at the church we attended, and I began to have doubts about my direction. I was in leadership in the church, but the pastor sometimes acted in ways that my wife and I felt were controlling. I took my new wife and the step-daughter that had been attending church with us and left. It was so hard because our recovery was tied to that church. I left bitter, and it took years to get over.

After we left, we bounced around from church to church. After my grandfather's house was sold, we also bounced around from living space to living space for many years.

In 2008, the housing bubble burst, and my job laid me off. I couldn't find work. We lived off Darlene's income and my unemployment payments, which wasn't much. I doubled down in school, but I struggled emotionally. I didn't like that I couldn't financially contribute. I knew God had a plan but what was happening seemed like a major setback.

Someone I knew in recovery told me that I should get my drug and alcohol counseling certification. I resisted at first because I didn't want to work as a professional counselor. I mentored people in recovery, but I wanted to do ministry. I didn't consider secular counseling to be a type of ministry. My options were nil, so while I was going to school double time, I also pursued the drug and alcohol counseling certification.

Darlene and I had found a small church under a new pastor. Because I wasn't working, I began struggling with my direction in life and trusting God. My wife was working herself to death while I finished school. The pastor encouraged me but made it plain that he didn't think God had called me to vocational ministry. He told me I tended to be quarrelsome and that elders in the church can't be quarrelsome. I think he also knew that I had trust issues with people; I had been through a lot.

When I realized that he wouldn't support my desire to pursue vocational ministry, I was confused and angry and eventually left that church. At one point, he had told me that I was good at working with people who are addicted; to go do that. At the time, it felt like rejection, but I believe now that this resistance was from God. The pastor was right; God had called me to a specific task. I eventually dedicated myself to one vocational purpose: substance use disorder and its associated problems.

I was very skeptical of people's motives, particularly pastors. His assessments of me were accurate. I was quarrelsome at times and overly suspicious of people's motivations. These traits are hindrances in the realm of ministry, which is all about connecting to others inside and outside the church.

In recovery, I have learned to manage the expression of these traits, but they are always under the surface. I am still hypervigilant to some extent. I still believe that God may use me for church ministry in the future but for now, He has given me a specific set of tasks related to my life experience and education.

In just over a year, I finished the drug and alcohol education, the internship, and passed the exam. This wouldn't have been possible if I had been working. I also obtained certificates in domestic violence, anger management, and the Nurturing Parenting Immersion Program that same year. I was nearly done with school, and I had met key people in various helping professions through my training and internships. Although the road getting there was rough, God began to open doors, and I began to see His plans.

After I became certified as a counselor, I couldn't find work, which is strange because there are always shortages of certified counselors. I was convinced that my criminal record had something to do with it. I prayed a lot. I was sure God had a plan, but I was also experiencing periods of doubt. Where was the God that I felt so close to when I left prison?

I attended the 40-hour domestic violence training through a local domestic violence agency earlier that year. Domestic violence and substance misuse are highly correlated, and I wanted to learn more. Out of the blue, one of the supervisors for the domestic violence agency set me up to do an internship in the domestic violence shelter. I had only spoken with her briefly once. Still, she asked me to volunteer to facilitate a group for victims who may have experienced substance misuse.

I have what is considered a violent felony, and males don't normally work in women's shelters. I asked her to confirm she wanted me to work in the shelter and reminded her that I was a male felon. She replied that we would see if it worked out. Shortly after, she offered me a job. It was mind-blowing to be given that opportunity. I believe God opened that door.

Working in the shelter was miserable though. I got the impression other workers were suspicious of me and I did not feel welcome. Eventually, I resigned but I completed my Bachelor of Arts in Christian Studies before I left. At my graduation, I walked Summa Cum Laude.

After I resigned from the job, I began struggling with confusion, frustration, and doubt. I picked myself up and began to apply for other jobs. I applied to Fresno County to be a Substance Abuse Specialist (SAS) and for the Substance Abuse Program Director at a local homeless service organization. I interviewed at the homeless service organization first, and they offered me the position the next day. The job offer lifted my spirits and gave me hope, but something told me to wait to respond to the offer. The next day Fresno County offered me the Substance Abuse Specialist job. The choice was a no-brainer; being a SAS for the county was a coveted position for local counselors. I took the county job, and they placed me at the Department of Social Services in Child Welfare. Working in Child Welfare launched my career.

Many people wait quite a while to get into the county. I felt God's hand expedited my progress in my profession. Once I was in

Child Welfare, I quickly understood why God had placed me at the domestic violence shelter. SASs in Fresno County Child Welfare services were required to review domestic violence assessments and refer parents to local agencies. Working in a shelter for a year gave me an understanding of domestic violence.

In Child Welfare, I discovered another gift God had given me: teaching and training. I had mentioned I would get high on drugs as a teen and read books. I read tons of college-level medical texts, books on mental health, addiction, the Physicians' Desk Reference, and many other topics. The knowledge I gained through books and my personal experience paired well with my natural ability to organize and articulate complex material.

I had a fantastic supervisor who encouraged professional growth and pushed me to train other workers internally, and so I did. It was stressful at first, but I received good reviews, and it boosted my confidence. While I was working in Child Welfare, I enrolled in a graduate program. My supervisor helped make special arrangements for me to get my practicum done at my workplace. I eventually earned a Master of Science in Addiction Counseling and graduated with a 4.0 GPA while working in Child Welfare. I credit her support.

My mom and my stepdad, who was sick with cancer at the time, watched me receive my graduate diploma. Finishing school and advancing in life were all my stepdad ever wanted for me. I praise God that he saw the fruit of his efforts and prayers before the Lord took him home. I am grateful that God provided me with a father to be there and celebrate with me.

Shortly before I left Child Welfare, my supervisor also allowed me to attend Social Worker Core Training which is only reserved for Child Welfare Social Workers. This training is mandated by the State of California. In this state region, Central California Training Academy (CCTA) conducts the training. The academy is associated with California State University, Fresno Foundation. I was only able to attend a few sessions before Child Welfare would no longer let me attend because I was not a social worker. But I participated in the right sessions, and I believe this also was God's providence.

There was a trainer who saw that I understood addiction and domestic violence. She was also a Christian. I told her I wanted to train social workers on certain topics. When I finished my graduate program, she and another academy employee helped bring me on as a contracted trainer for Child Welfare Social Workers in twelve counties. Seven years later, I still train for CCTA on the topics of substance use disorder, intimate partner violence, behavioral health, and trauma-informed practice.

The extra finances carried Darlene and me through hard times. Eventually, my wife had to leave cosmetology to have surgeries on her hand because of work-related tendon problems. She could no longer cut hair and had to do something else. She went back to school to earn her Bachelor of Business Administration degree. During the time she wasn't working, once again, we didn't have much money.

My wife and I dreamed of homeownership, but we always ran into troubles. Our finances were impacted by job loss, time in school, work related injuries, and Darlene was diagnosed with cancer but God brought us through all these safely and worked every hardship to our advantage. Eventually, Fresno County hired my wife as an Account Clerk. She developed relationships in her department that helped to elevate her career. She ultimately became a Staff Analyst for Fresno County. Today, she is a Staff Analyst in Human Resources with a special district in Fresno County.

Shortly after I finished my graduate program and began training for CCTA, I transferred from Child Welfare to the Fresno County Department of Behavioral Health. Working in Child Welfare was difficult but the most educational experience of my career. When you work in Child Welfare you learn in dog years about human problems because they all show up there. It was a stressful place to work in general, but it was hard for me for other reasons. These parents struggled with the same issues that I had before the miracle happened in my life. It was rewarding in many respects, but the parent's stories also reminded me of my past. Despite the stress and heartbreak that I saw there, I value the experience it gave me, but it was time to leave.

The Department of Behavioral Health assigned me to a unit of treatment program reviewers. Now I was learning about the regulatory side of the addiction treatment profession. Every year, the SASs on the team would attend conferences for drug and alcohol counselors. At one conference, I ran into the CEO of the California Consortium of Addiction Programs and Professionals (CCAPP). CCAPP is the most prominent alcohol and drug counseling certifying organization in California. They are also a powerful advocacy organization and education provider. When I was getting my drug and alcohol counselor certification, I hoped to be involved with CCAPP at the board level.

For a brief time, I was a CCAPP academy instructor. I had met the CEO before, but it wasn't a positive meeting. It was my fault. I had said something I shouldn't have. When he saw me at the conference, he approached me to tell me how he felt. We spent time talking it out. That evening, he called me and asked if I wanted to go to dinner, which was unexpected.

When I went downstairs to meet him, he told me that we were going to dinner with one of my industry heroes. I was so excited I could hardly contain myself. It was a fantastic experience, but it got even better. A few months later, the CEO called and asked if I wanted to be on the CCAPP board. I jumped on it. I knew this was God because I had never expressed my desire to be on the CCAPP board to anyone. Only God knew this.

At the Department of Behavioral Health, I was promoted to Senior Substance Abuse Specialist but eventually transitioned into a Staff Analyst position, overseeing substance use disorder prevention. Early on during my employment with the Department of Behavioral Health, they found out that I was a trainer. My deputy director called me into the office, and I presented her with foundational training materials that I put together on substance use disorder. She was a tremendous support because I was allowed to deliver the training countywide. Over the next six years, I trained social workers, job specialists, mental health therapists, recreational therapists, physicians, nurses, nursing students, pharmacy students, religious organizations, police officers, and educators on the topic of substance use disorder.

About a year into my time at the Department of Behavioral Health, I reviewed a treatment program at the Juvenile Justice Center. There is an organization located at the center called Focus Forward that helps case manage incarcerated youth back into the community. Every few years, they published a magazine with stories of hope—stories of people who had experienced trouble in their lives but ended up turning their lives around. I told them that I would like to tell my story.

A year later, they contacted me for an interview and a photo shoot. A few months later, they informed me that I would be the cover story. I was blown away. That magazine was distributed all over Fresno, and people began to recognize me. The Department of Behavioral Health also used me to create media messaging on substance misuse and addiction which I continue to do. Essentially, I became the primary department representative for media interviews, live town halls, and public service announcements on topics related to alcohol and drugs.

In my second year on the CCAPP board (2017), I was elected Vice-President of the Board of Directors. In my third year, I was elected President. The following year, I was re-elected board Vice-President and was appointed as Legislative Chair.

I have also written articles for Counselor Magazine, provided input on proposed bill language, testified to the California State Assembly on proposed legislation, and traveled to Washington DC to meet with prominent addiction-focused organizations, such as the American Society of Addiction Medicine (ASAM), and the Office of National Drug Control Policy (ONDCP). I even had the opportunity to speak directly with one legislator as well as other staffers about addiction and industry-related issues.

In 2020, California State University, Fresno hired me as an adjunct professor in the Criminology Department. In 2021, I pursued the Substance Abuse Professional (SAP) credential to work with Department of Transportation (DOT) regulated employees. I am the owner of Covenant Training and Consulting, which offers alcohol and drug assessment, individual and family education, and consultation to the public on substance use, misuse, and addiction.

My career path has been a fantastic journey, but my family life is even better. My marriage to my wife has grown deeper over the years. I am convinced that before her, I never truly knew what love was. She is good at loving me and I think I am pretty good at loving her back. My son and I have a good relationship today as well. He lives in Philadelphia with his mother, but I see him periodically throughout the year. I also have a good relationship with my step-daughters. I even walked one of them down the aisle at her wedding. The wedding took place at the same church, at the same altar where I had encountered God as a child and later as an adult.

Best of all, I have four grandchildren: two boys and two girls. My grandsons recently moved out of state, but that gives me a reason to travel in the future. My granddaughters are close to home, and I get to watch them grow. I own a home today as well. God knew the life I wanted. He understood the desires of my heart and granted them to me.

The bottom line is that I am happy in God's care. I worked hard to get here, but I know God did this for me. He opened the doors, created opportunities, and prepared me for the life that he had for me. Even though the journey involved pain, I experienced post-traumatic growth and blessing far beyond what I deserve. Through my pain and triumph, I obtained some of the wisdom I prayed so hard for as a young teenager.

Today I am working on 17 years of continuous sobriety. My heart's desire was just to be well and to function normally. I was sick for so many years. All of my doctors claimed that I was mentally ill. They attributed the illness to chemical imbalances in my brain and to trauma. They attempted to adjust my brain chemistry through medication and informed me I would need the medication for the rest of my life. The medicine didn't fix my pain. It only worked to stabilize me enough to function, and some of the abusable medications they prescribed me exacerbated my addiction.

The professionals who had to deal with me interpreted my problems and applied solutions they were trained to use, but they missed me in the process. Pastors told me my sole problem was that I had a sinful nature and a wicked heart. Psychiatrists viewed me as a chemically imbalanced biological machine. Therapists viewed my symptoms through a lens of childhood trauma and environmental influences. Law enforcement viewed me through the lens of criminogenic needs. Educators just seemed to view me as a child in need of discipline.

I believe all these lenses provided some accurate insights into Michael. Still, none of them could help on their own because they could only see part of the picture. A multitude of factors caused my symptoms, but nobody took the time to truly get to know me. People tried to help me, but they gave up on me when they couldn't make progress. In the end, human efforts had a limited impact, and God intervened to save my life and restore me. God knew me. God never gave up on me.

I honestly do not think that there is a scientific explanation for how I got well and how I continue to stay well. However, one must ask, how does a man who suffered significant childhood trauma, mental illness, and drug dependency for decades, who everyone wrote off as hopeless, enter prison in the worst state he has ever been in, get sent to the worst possible place for recovery, and come out completely well if God didn't do it?

My family members and people who know me remained stunned as they continued to watch all of this unfold. Mental health and substance use disorder treatment gave me tools and provided temporary assistance when needed but could never address the core issues. They couldn't heal me.

It wasn't until God encountered me and intervened did the healing happen, and my dreams for the future came to pass. God penetrated my hard heart, mended the brokenness, sparked a fire in it, then gave me a purpose that has propelled me forward. He has given me something I thought was unattainable, something that nothing and nobody else could ever give. God has given me joy and contentment. My life was darkness, but now it's full of light. I can see it. God does this. With God, all things are possible.

What the pastor told me was true: God is, God hears, and God delivers. I am not just functioning; I am thriving. I am not just well; I am better than well.

# CHAPTER 12:

## The Freeing Power of Truth

*"Then you will know the truth, and truth will set you free."*
*(John 8:32, NIV)*

*"Jesus replied, 'Very truly I tell you, everyone who sins is
a slave to sin. Now a slave has no permanent place in the
family, but a son belongs to it forever. So if the Son sets
you free, you will be free indeed.'"(John 8:34-36, NIV)*

Early on in this book, I said my story ultimately begins and ends with God. I hope that you, as the reader, were able to see God on display as He watched over and interjected Himself into my life at strategic times to bring about the life I currently live.

The most vivid display of God's work in my life is seen in chapter 10 as He dealt with me in prison by convicting me of my sinful behavior, correcting my perspective, healing the injuries in my life caused by others and myself, and renewing my relationship with Him. As the author of the story, trying to put myself into the mind of the reader, I can imagine perhaps some may be wondering how this could be possible. How can prayer and reading an ancient religious book (the Bible) bring people closer to God and result in healing for so many?

It sometimes seems like a mystery to me as well, except I can say that it happened to me. I am convinced that I was literally touched by God in a miraculous way, but the change happened in tandem with prayer and Bible reading. Given God's power to change lives through the scriptures, it's hard to imagine that the Bible can be anything other than what the authors of the Bible claim it is: the inspired word of God. I am convinced that it is. In the book of 2 Timothy, chapter 3, verse 16 of the Bible it says:

*"All scripture is God-breathed and is useful for teaching, rebuking, correcting, and training in righteousness." (NIV)*

The Bible puts God's righteousness on display. It shows us who God is, what humans were meant to be, what our current condition is, and the plan for our redemption.

If you read through the verses God used to reach me in chapter 10 and thought they were harsh, I can relate. I remember growing up in churches that gave me a very lopsided view of God.

I knew God was righteous and I always knew, but as hard as I tried, I could never meet God's perfect standard. I had never understood how grace bridged the gap between God's perfection and my imperfection.

Our inability to meet God's standards is why we need redemption. I am convinced the main reason that I was terrified of God, despite His care and protection over my life, was because I wasn't adequately taught about the love and grace of God eternally displayed in the gospel of Jesus. Gospel means good news, but to grasp the good news, we do need to understand the bad news: our true condition.

From the very beginning, the Bible declares the universe and everything within it was created by God. This includes our little planet and all the life on it.

*"In the beginning God created the heavens and the earth. Now the earth was formless and empty, darkness was over the surface of*

*the deep, and the Spirit of God was hovering over the waters."*
*(Genesis 1:1-2, NIV)*

*"Then God said, "Let us make mankind in our image, in our like ness, so that they may rule over the fish in the sea and the birds in the sky, over the livestock and all the wild animals, and over all the creatures that move along the ground. So God created mankind in his own image, in the image of God he created them; male and female he created them." (Genesis 1:26-27, NIV)*

The Bible is clear that the plan for human beings was an intimate connection with God and eternal life and peace. The first created man and woman, our representatives, rebelled against God and disobeyed. They didn't stay within the parameters God established for their own protection. The Bible calls this rebellious disobedience sin. Sin simply means missing the mark. The consequences of that sin were catastrophic.

With this one act of disobedience, the intimate connection to God was broken for them and for all of us who descended from them. This intimate connection to God was the steering mechanism for their life and ours. The hearts of people became corrupted.

Most importantly, this disobedience led to the physical death of the body and spiritual death, eternal separation from God, for eternity.

The brokenness caused by sin made it impossible for us to have true intimacy with God on our own. *"God is light; in him there is no darkness at all"* (1 John 1:5, NIV). Our hearts became dark. Darkness and light cannot dwell together.

The self-centered, self-reliant, God-rejecting disposition of our hearts expresses itself in a variety of ways. In the book of Romans, in the Bible, chapter 1, verses 28-32 say:

*"Furthermore, just as they did not think it worthwhile to retain the knowledge of God, so God gave them over to a depraved mind, so that they do what ought not to be done. They have become filled with every kind of wickedness, evil, greed and depravity. They are full of envy, murder, strife, deceit and malice. They are gossips, slanderers, God-haters, insolent, arrogant and boastful; they invent ways of doing evil; they disobey their parents; they have no understanding, no fidelity, no love, no mercy. Although they know God's righteous decree that those who do such things deserve death, they not only continue to do these very things but also approve of those who practice them."*
*(NIV)*

In short, we attempt to do it *our way*. Because men and women were created to have a relationship with God, the absence of that relationship left an internal void, a void we constantly try to fill. People attempt to substitute God's good gifts for God himself. We walk around hungry for something we can't find..., something that is just out of reach, whether that something is a new car, relationship, career, or a fix. What we need, what will satisfy that hunger, is a restored relationship with our Creator. In our quest to find fulfillment and soothe the emptiness in our souls, we inadvertently create a god who meets our qualifications. We want a god that makes us comfortable; one who affirms us no matter how we choose to live. Sometimes we reject the idea of God altogether and try to make ourselves the ultimate authority over our lives.

When we believe and put our faith in something other than who God says He is, it is essentially what the Bible terms idolatry or the worship of something that isn't God.

To top it off, we are blind. Without help, we can't see our own condition. There is a partial willfulness to our spiritual blindness, a type of malignant denial of truth. Even though humans exist in this state, and don't know much about God until God reveals himself to us individually, the Bible declares that we know enough. We see creation all around us and feel a standard for human behavior within us and when we don't respond to what we know we are accountable for that. The book of Romans in the Bible, chapter 1, verses 18-21 and 25 state:

*"The wrath of God is being revealed from heaven against all the godlessness and wickedness of people, who suppress the truth by their wickedness, since what may be known about God is plain to them, because God has made it plain to them. For since the creation of the world God's invisible qualities-his eternal power and divine nature-have been clearly seen, being understood from what has been made, so that people are without excuse. For although they knew God, they neither glorified him as God nor gave thanks to him, but their thinking became futile, and their foolish hearts were darkened." (NIV)*

*"They exchanged the truth about God for a lie and worshiped and served created things rather than the Creator—who is forever praised. Amen." (NIV)*

In my observation, I have noticed people strongly cling to the idea that humans are basically good. At least many of us believe we are, even if we think the person next to us might not be. There is no arguing that some of us are better than others, but the belief that we are basically good makes people feel that God, as He truly is, is unnecessary or that God approves of our lives as they are. Our tendency to have a low standard of good, as well as our tendency to compare ourselves to others who we perceive as worse than we are, does not help us when it comes to God because God's standards are higher than ours.

If we do not deny the existence of God outright, we then tend to make God into our own likeness, assuming He thinks and judges the world as we do. This is a grave error. God is far greater and entirely other. Our fallen and corrupted condition prevents us from seeing how needy we are.

A sense of morality has been built into us since creation, an echo of our Creator. We know when we do wrong much of the time. This is the reason so many of us strongly feel guilt, shame, and unease in the world and don't exactly know why.

When God opens the eyes of a person so they can see, we can call that a spiritual awakening. God supernaturally gives a person the ability to see their true condition and their need for salvation, allowing them to understand and accept God's provision of grace in the person and work of Jesus. He then sustains them in a continuing relationship with Himself which leads to ongoing spiritual growth.

God can reach a person using different means and at different points in their life but coming to salvation always begins with a conviction and acknowledgment that the person has sinned against God. It's followed by a confession of their sinfulness and an asking for forgiveness. It ends with them putting their faith in God's gift of salvation offered in the gospel of Jesus Christ.

For me, this happened as a child, but in the end, God needed to break through the rebellious, angry, and resentful attitudes of my heart so that I could ultimately experience His love and grace fully as an adult. God let my pain and sinful choices run their course to bring me to a place of surrender and then used my experiences to help others. This story was a glimpse into how God dealt with me specifically over time. It isn't necessarily the way that God handles all His children. God deals very gently with people as well. If you are a parent, you know children are all very different and we deal with them individually, even though the rules of the house apply to them all. But even though we deal with children individually, the common denominator is that they are all sons or daughters with family privileges.

The question then is, how does a person become a son or daughter of God? This is the most important question anyone can ask themselves and the essence of the gospel of Jesus which is all about redemption and adoption.

When I heard the gospel at 8 years old, I believed it and I put my faith in Jesus. I was adopted by God as a son. Did I stay the course and follow God perfectly after that? Obviously not. For many years, I went through hard times and was rebellious, but God continuously drew me back to himself, eventually leading to the powerful God encounter in prison that resulted in more permanent change.

It was the internal identification with God as my Father when I was young that made me respond to His constant calls throughout my life even when I was still wounded, immature, and acting like a fool. I was adopted as a son when I was little and even though I didn't act like a son (and still don't at times), I was a son nonetheless, and as an adopted child of God, He corrected me like one.

Before I go into the gospel, I want to reiterate something important, and it's often hard for people to accept. Many people think that by virtue of being human we are automatically sons and daughters of God. After all, He created us, right? The Bible says we were created in God's image. We certainly have abilities and characteristics that separate us from other created things on the planet. Despite the wide variety of wicked traits we display, I think most would agree that there is a dignity that comes with being a human. We feel a sense of human dignity because we were stamped with God's image at creation but as the Bible verses that I included earlier in the chapter reveal, our relationship with God was broken, and the image of God's likeness was and continues to be marred by sin. Any opportunity for a relationship with God would have to be restored.

Due to our natural hostility toward God and blindness to our own condition, it would have to be God who would plan and initiate the restorative process, and He did that, which brings me to the gospel or good news of Jesus.

It's important to note right away the Bible declares that God loves humanity deeply. God's love for us cannot be overstated. God went to great lengths to give people the opportunity to be restored to Him when He could have done something entirely different. I want to convey God's love because there are many who struggle with the concept of God as loving because of all the pain and suffering in the world. I know I struggled with it and sometimes still do. Our suffering is real and often embitters us, but the Bible is clear from the beginning that suffering in the world is a consequence of original sin, humanity's fallen nature, and our own sin.

Often, we are hurt by others, or suffer from an illness that isn't our fault, but even those things are symptomatic of the fallen, broken world in which we live. Evil and death operate in the world. I used to rage against God and blame Him because of the pain I experienced but God showed me the bigger picture as I read the Bible and clarified the plan of restoration to me. God is love and can restore us to Himself at the asking. God provided a way back to Him through the work of His son Jesus. In the book of John, chapter 3, verses 16-17 say:

> *"For God so loved the world that he gave his one and only Son, that whoever believes in him shall not perish but have eternal life. For God didn't send his Son into the world to condemn the world, but to save the world through him. Whoever believes in him isn't condemned, but whoever does not believe stands condemned already because they have not believed in the name of God's one and only Son." (NIV).*

These familiar verses reveal the gospel of Jesus and show the heart of God, though I want to unpack it a little. The verse makes it clear that God loves the world, and His intention is the salvation, reconciliation, and restoration of people. In fact, the Bible declares that God is love and love has characteristics. The book of 1 Corinthians, chapter 13, verses 4-8 say:

*"Love is patient, love is kind. It does not envy, it does not boast, it is not proud. It does not dishonor others, it is not self-seeking, it is not easily angered, it keeps no record of wrongs. Love does not delight in evil but rejoices with the truth. It always protects, always trusts, always hopes, always perseveres. Love never fails."* (NIV)

As you can see in the verses, patience, and kindness, which would include mercy and forgiveness, are key components of love. But it also says love cannot delight in evil and rejoices with the truth. Love cannot overlook evil. Justice is a characteristic of love as well. God, being love, wants to show humans kindness, mercy, and forgiveness but overlooking sin and leaving wrongdoing unpunished would be unjust, unloving, and inconsistent with His character. God cannot be anything other than what He is. In the book of Malachi, chapter 3, verse 6, it says:

*"I the LORD do not change."* (NIV)

Sin is a serious problem. The book of Romans in the Bible, chapter 6, verse 23 says:

*"For the wages of sin is death, but the gift of God is eternal life in Christ Jesus our Lord."* (NIV)

Further, Romans 3:23 says:

*"For all have sinned and fall short of the glory of God." (NIV)*

If the penalty of sin is death and all have sinned, then we are all under a death sentence. This seems like a major dilemma. God is equally merciful and just. How can God show mercy to sinners without compromising justice? How can God execute justice for sinful acts without neglecting mercy? God cannot compromise His own character.

The only solution to the dilemma would be if sin could be paid for another way, by a substitute. The substitute would have to be perfect and flawless. The substitute couldn't be tainted by sin and wrongdoing, or it would not be acceptable. So, who could be that substitute? It couldn't be one of us because we are all sinful and corrupt. None of us could ever repay the debt we owe for our own sins, let alone the sin debt of all people. The substitute would have to be perfect like God himself and only one fits that description. God's substitute was His Son, Jesus. The book of Hebrews in the Bible, chapter 1, verses 1-3, provides an amazing description of Jesus and His work of human redemption:

*"In the past God spoke to our ancestors through the prophets at many times and in various ways, but in these last days he has spoken to us by his Son, whom he appointed heir of all things, and through whom also he made the universe. The Son is the radiance of God's glory and the exact representation of his being, sustaining all things by his powerful word. After he had provided purification for sins, he sat down at the right hand of the Majesty in heaven." (NIV)*

The Bible declares that Jesus is the eternal Son of God. He was with God, His father, for all eternity past. In fact, the Bible describes God as Father, Son, and Holy Spirit. As the verse above states, the universe was created through Jesus. He is divine and wasn't created like one of us. Jesus always was, but He came into the world as one of us. John 3:16, the verse I included earlier, stated … "He gave his one and only son." God gave Jesus as a gift to humanity.

The Bible says that Jesus was born of a virgin conceived by God. He became a man, but unlike us, He lived a perfect, sinless life even though He was tempted to sin as we are. He perfectly kept God's law and performed miracles, signs and wonders to demonstrate to the world that He is the Son of God.

The Bible testifies that despite His sinless perfection, He was falsely accused of wrongdoing, and even though no accusations could be substantiated, He was crucified on the cross as a sinless, innocent man. It wasn't by accident; this was the plan from eternity past.

Jesus came to reveal God to us and take the punishment we deserve for the wrongs we have done to satisfy justice so that God could show mercy to those who would believe and put their faith in Jesus for salvation.

God poured out His wrath for sin on Jesus so He could pour out His mercy on those who would believe. Sin, death, and separation from God came into the world through the first human man but righteousness, life, and salvation came into the world through Jesus. Because Jesus was perfect and fulfilled the law of God, His death was able to wipe out the sin debt of all who would come to God through faith in Him.

It wasn't just His death as a substitute for us that is important. If all Jesus did was die as we die, we would still have no hope for redemption and eternal life. The Bible says that He was buried after His crucifixion and raised from the dead on the third day, defeating death.

After His resurrection, He appeared to hundreds of people and then ascended to the right hand of God. The resurrection indicated that the sacrifice for our sin was acceptable, sufficient, and complete.

The resurrection is also a foreshadowing of the eternal life to come for all of us who believe and put our faith in Him.

So, how does a person obtain salvation? Believe. Trust. Accept the payment for sin on your behalf. Too easy? It's called grace and it's free a gift to us, though it cost the giver a great deal. The book of Romans, chapter 10, verse 9 says:

*"If you declare with your mouth, "Jesus is Lord," and believe in your heart that God raised him from the dead, you will be saved." (NIV)*

The Bible says that those who put their faith in Jesus, pass from death to life. Though we all die physically, we can have the assurance that we will spend eternity with God. Not only is our sin debt wiped clean and eternal life secured by Jesus' death and resurrection for those who believe, but also, God gives us Jesus' righteousness.

In other words, those who put their faith in Jesus are seen as perfect before God as though they have never done wrong. However, the blessing that God pours out on us does not end there. When we put our faith in Jesus, we are also given the Holy Spirit to dwell within us. Our nature is changed. While we may still sin because we still have much of our old nature, our natural inclination toward sinful behavior begins to diminish as God begins to conform us into the image of Jesus. God gives us a new nature. Where we didn't have an interest in spiritual things pertaining to God, we gain it. Life takes on new meaning and we are free to live for God in service to others as we were created to do.

In short, we become less selfish and learn to love and experience God's care and presence in our lives which leads to joy and contentment. Jesus did what we could never do on our own. He created a way in which we could have fellowship with God again by removing the barrier of sin and punishment, but the Bible makes clear Jesus is the only way to restoration. No other provision for reconciliation and salvation was made by God. In the book of John, chapter 14, verse 6, Jesus himself says:

> *"I am the way and the truth and the life. No one comes*
> *to the Father except through me." (NIV)*

Referring to Jesus, the book of Acts, chapter 4, verse 12 says:

> *"Salvation is found in no one else, for there is no other name under*
> *heaven given to mankind by which we must be saved." (NIV)*

1 Timothy, chapter 2, verse 5-6 says:

> *"For there is one God and one mediator between God and mankind,*
> *the man Christ Jesus, who gave himself as a ransom for all people."*
> *(NIV)*

A greater understanding of this salvation through Jesus is what came to me in prison. The miraculous change in my life didn't just happen because the Bible confronted my sin. That was just the first step toward change. If that had been all, I would have felt worse and probably driven to deeper despair, but the Bible reminded me of God's solution for providing forgiveness and reconciliation through Jesus. It was a truth I had known, experienced, possessed, and believed since childhood but never fully understood.

When I asked for forgiveness and surrendered my life to Jesus in prison, I was empowered to let go of my old way of living. God freed me from the bondage of sinful behavior that was killing me and renewed the faith that guides my life. Because of the sacrifice Jesus made, eternity with God awaits me. Not because of anything good I do, but because of what He did for me.

Though I am far from perfect and tend to drift into bad behavior at times, God does not let me stay there. God's patience and loving-kindness are always on display in my life as He corrects me and draws me back to himself. When that happens my faith in God increases. I am still a man under construction, but I am not the man I was. The transformation that happened in my life is evidence of the truth and power of the message of the gospel and my story is one of the myriads of other stories across time and across the globe.

The love of God I felt in prison healed my mental health issues and made alcohol and drugs no longer necessary. Guilt and shame were lifted off my shoulders so that I could live free.

Forgiveness, salvation, restoration, joy, and contentment are there for all who put their faith in Jesus and trust Him for salvation. It is a gift with no strings. When we put our faith in Jesus, we are adopted into God's family and the Holy Spirit begins to transform us.

All we must do is surrender and ask Jesus to come into our lives and make a change. Jesus is true hope for the future and care for the present. The book of Matthew in the Bible, chapter 7, verses 7-8 say:

*"Ask and it will be given to you; seek and you will find; knock and the door will be opened to you. For everyone who asks receives; the one who seeks finds; and to the one who knocks, the door will be opened."*
*(NIV)*

In the book of John in the Bible, chapter 6, verses 37, Jesus says:

*"All those the Father gives me will come to me, and whoever comes to me I will never drive away." (NIV)*

When I set out to write this book, my goal was to put God on display so that people would know that God reaches out to human-ity to save and restore people. Perhaps, you read this book and, like me, you have known the truth but drifted away from it. Or perhaps maybe this is the first time you have been exposed to the gospel of Jesus and you feel the Spirit of God tugging at your heart, telling you to turn from your current way of life and believe in Jesus. I want the reader to know, and I hope my story demonstrates the truth that it does not matter how far away from God a person may feel, and it does not matter what they have done in the past, God's love and forgiveness through Jesus overcomes all obstacles. God is always available. I hope this story strengthened the faith of those who already believe in and trust Jesus, and I hope this story inspires those who do not know Jesus to seek Him. God bless.

# APPENDIX I:
## Amends & Forgiveness

In the Christian life and the recovery process, I learned the importance of making amends with people who I hurt whenever it was possible. Even though I know God has forgiven me, it does not free me from the necessity of seeking to repair the damage that I had done in the past. After all, God is for reconciliation in relationships.

In the early years of my sobriety, I made significant efforts to seek the forgiveness of those I wronged but it was not always possible. While it is important to seek forgiveness, I was also taught that I should not do so if there was a possibility of injuring myself or others in the process. Some people in my past told me plainly that they never want to have contact with me again. With others, I assumed that was the case. I wanted to respect their wishes and their space. As a result, I never approached them.

To complicate matters further, I am certain that I could never recall all the events that might warrant an amends. Some people who I injured I never personally met. Others have passed on. So, what does a person do when amends cannot be made, and forgiveness cannot be sought from others?

In recovery, we are encouraged to make a "living amends" of our lives. For me, this means that I orient my life in such a way that I am living for the good of the people in my life and the general community in the form of lifelong service. I hope that as you read the story, you can see that my life is a living amends today and has been for more than 16 years.

With that being said, I do not want to miss the opportunity to seek the forgiveness of people I may never speak to again. If you are reading this book, and you were hurt by me in any way, I want to express to you how very sorry I am for any injury I caused and ask that you forgive me. If not for my sake, for your own. The man I used to be is not worth being resentful toward. I am well aware of the fact that I do not deserve the restored life that God has given me. I am what I am today by His grace and nothing more.

In addition, I also offer my forgiveness for those that caused me injury in the past. I hold no ill will and pray that you find God's grace as I have.

# APPENDIX II:
## A Christian Mother's Heart

When I read the manuscript for my son Michael's book, I understood his purpose in writing it but, I must admit, it brought me no small measure of pain. I realized, however, that I would not be the true recipient of God's grace that He called me to be if I wasn't willing to support the telling of his story—even if it meant reliving those painful years.

If you've read far enough in the book to be reading this, you've no doubt already learned the details of Michael's story—many of which I did not know until I read about them here. Some of those accounts cast many of the adults in his life in a less than favorable light—including myself. Michael assures me that this wasn't his intention but that he needed to highlight the events that impacted him early on to tell the story. I can honestly say that we did the best we could under very difficult circumstances and today Michael and I have a good relationship.

I've titled this *A Mother's Heart* because in supporting my son's purpose for this book I want my heart's desire, which is honoring God, to be known. I was a very young single mother of two and felt very insecure in that role from the start, but when Michael's behavioral issues began around the age of 6, those feelings of insecurity quickly turned to despair. So much so, that I wouldn't have made it had it not been for the love of Christ and other people God placed in my life—my family, my church, my friends, and my loving husband of 30 years, Orville.

The issues in Michael's early life included being kicked out of several schools, mental health struggles, alcohol and drug abuse, wrecking every car he ever owned, and culminated in his incarceration at Soledad State Prison. I made many mistakes along that journey for which I take responsibility, but when things were at their worst I reached out to God. I told Him, "Lord, I'm losing this boy!" And I heard Him say, "Helen, he's not yours to lose, he's mine. He came into the world through you, but he belongs to me, so let me have him."

So, I gave my son completely over to God and wrote to Michael in prison telling him I was done. As a mother, those were the hardest words I had ever written, but spiritually they brought me the greatest peace I had felt since Michael's troubles began. At last, I was giving my son over completely to the only one who could help him and, as you've read, Michael's story ends as a testament to God's grace, mercy, and love, and demonstrates God's absolute sovereign authority over His children. I will never cease to praise Him for it.

So, if you're a parent, grandparent, friend, or loved one of a person who is lost and addicted, I say, even if we can't help them, don't give up because God can!

Just as you can trust God for your salvation (and I pray you have or that you will), also trust God for theirs. Please take your children to church and give them a strong foundation of faith that God can build upon and use in times of crisis.

> *"Start children off on the way they should go, and even when they are old they will not turn from it." (Proverbs 22:6, NIV)*

Let me encourage you with truth from God's word just as it has encouraged this mother's heart!

*"And he who searches our hearts knows the mind of the Spirit,
because the Spirit intercedes for God's people in accordance with the
will of God. And we know that in all things God works for the good of
those who love him, who have been called according to his purpose."*
(Romans 8:27-28, NIV)

*"Trust in the LORD with all your heart and lean not on your own
understanding; in all your ways submit to him, and he
will make your paths straight." (Proverbs 3:5-6, NIV)*

*"For I know the plans I have for you," declares the LORD,
"plans to prosper you and not to harm you, plans to
give you hope and a future." (Jeremiah 29:11, NIV)*

Finally, because our Lord and Savior turned a life that was
nearly destroyed into a blessing, it is this mother's prayer that as you
read this book, the Lord will use our trials to prevent or free you
from yours. Know that the Lord can bestow…

*"….a crown of beauty instead of ashes, the oil of joy instead of
mourning, and a garment of praise instead of a spirit of despair.
They will be called oaks of righteousness, a planting of the
Lord for the display of his splendor." (Isaiah 61:3, NIV)*

**~ Helen Lewis (Michael's Mother)**

# APPENDIX III:
## Dedication

Ultimately, I am dedicating this book to the Lord Jesus Christ, who accomplished in me what medical science and its treatments could never accomplish on their own. However, human beings also played critical roles in my life along the way. Many of them are mentioned in the acknowledgment section of this book, but I want to dedicate this book to three special people in my life: my son Gabriel Prichard, my wife Darlene Prichard, and my mother Helen Lewis.

Gabriel,

This book is first dedicated to you because it was written for you. It was in my heart to write my story for you even before I decided I would publish a book. I wrote it because first and foremost I love you, but also because I wanted you to have a history of my life and what God did for me and ultimately for you. One of the greatest pains I experienced in my life was the loss of your grandfather David; I never really knew him. I did not want that to be the case in your life. I want you to know your father not only through our personal interactions but through the narrative of this story so you will always have my testimony with you. I know I have told you this before, but God giving you to me saved my life. My love for you and the love that I knew you had for me caused me to hang on to hope when my life was utter darkness. You are precious to me son, a gift from heaven and an expression of God's love toward all who know you. Thank you for always forgiving my parental shortcomings. I know they have been many. I want you to know that I am proud of you and what you have accomplished in life so far, and I trust that God has more good things for you in the future. You are the best son a man could hope for. I love you.

Darlene,

This book is dedicated to you not just because you're my wife but because you have been my biggest support for the 15 years of our lives together. When I prayed for a wife while in recovery, God chose you. Your love is a blessing from God. You and I are a perfect match. God knew it would be hard rebuilding our individual lives after the trauma we both experienced and through so many years of drug addiction, so He gave us each other to ease the burden of having to recover alone. In our marriage, we have had to endure spiritual, family, health, and financial hardships; but we trusted God and loved each other through it. God has been faithful to us over the years and has blessed us with joy, contentment, and stability, which includes loving children and grandchildren. We could have never accomplished all that we have accomplished without each other and without God's oversight. I am praying that God grants us many more happy years together. I could write a book on the joys of being married to you, but I want to end by saying this: I never knew it was possible to love a woman so intensely. Your love is the most visible and tangible manifestation of God's love and grace in my life daily. You are my greatest earthly asset and my truest friend. I love you.

Mother,

I am dedicating this book to you because I am grateful for the love and care you provided me over the years. This story is as much about your pain and struggle as it is about mine. I came into this world through you, so we have been in this together from the beginning. I knew that in reading this story you would be forced to relive pain you wanted to forget, and you would learn things about my experience that you did not want to know. I knew in telling this story there would be parts that might unintentionally place you in a negative light. I also knew that I would not be able to effectively balance the negativity with all the positive aspects of who you are or be able to include a description of all the pain you went through, trying to carry the weight of your own suffering, my addiction, and other family problems.

So, it is a testament to your character that you gave your blessing to the publication of this book in the hope that it might help others. I know that you, like all parents, have struggled with what you could have done differently in your parenting, but the truth is you were a young, struggling mother with pain of your own to carry and under the circumstances, I know you did your best and your best helped get me to where I am today.

In all that we went through, I knew that you loved me. You often told me so, you showed me physical affection, you made sure my needs and many of my wants were met, and most importantly you instilled knowledge of God in me which ultimately saved my life. I know for certain that the pain I caused you far outweighs any pain you may have unintentionally caused me. I know that you agonized over me, lost sleep because of me, and pleaded constantly with God on my behalf. I was a victim of your prayers and God being who He is, answered them. With all the prayers that went up for me, I did not stand a chance of remaining unwell. We came out of those hard times because the Lord watched over us and now those dark days are over.

God's grace was upon you as you carried out your role as my mother even if there were mistakes, and the truth is, you are the unsung hero of my story. Proverbs 31:28 says, "Her children arise and call her blessed; her husband also, and he praises her:" (NIV).

You are a blessing in the lives of all who know you. Thank you for your perseverance. I love you.

# APPENDIX IV:
## Acknowledgements

**Personal Supports**

To my grandmothers, Alice Smith and Shirley Prichard, who are with the Lord. They loved me and helped raise me when my mother was struggling as a single mom. Their love and care provided a sense of stability when life was turbulent.

To my maternal grandfather, Roger Smith, who is with the Lord. He taught me how to fish and made time for me as a child.

To my stepfather, Orville Williams, who is with the Lord. He provided for me, prayed for me, and loved me like I was his own.

To my sister, Jennifer Prichard, you offered kindness and support to my son and me even when I was not well. Your dedication during those times was God-sent.

To my aunt, Margaret Venckeleer, you prayed for me, supported my mom, and made significant attempts to help the family get to the bottom of my struggles. You are and have always been a rock in the family.

To Patti Muscarella, you prayed for me, loved me through the years, never treated me differently when I was not well, and have been a cheerleader for me in my recovery.

To Sandra Ramage, God used you to bless me in so many ways over the years. I wouldn't even know where to begin. I will never forget your kindness.

To my stepdaughter, Danielle Burt, you supported your mother and me in recovery, helped us both get through school, and gave us two wonderful grandsons. You are a blessing.

To my stepdaughter, Breanna Rubitski, you are always there when your mother and I need you and you gave us two adorable granddaughters. I appreciate you so much.

To Carol and Ralph King, you helped Darlene and me in our recovery and instilled the character that lives in Darlene, Danielle, and Breanna, and is currently forming in Caiden, Giselle, Owen, and Auria. Thank you for your support.

## Supports for Book Completion

To my editor, Shawna Guzman, your wisdom, and input helped guide the creation of this book. Thank you so much for taking on this project, praying over it, and helping me produce a cohesive narrative.

To my stepdaughter, Danielle Burt, thank you for helping me put the finishing touches on the book.

To my uncle, Lauren Smith (Lauren Smith Brand Communications), thank you so much for taking the time to help design the cover. Your contributions helped to capture the spirit of the book.

To Brian Bishop (Brian Bishop Photography), thank you for taking the photo for the back cover of the book.

To Mia Clark, you have been a huge supporter of this book and strongly encouraged its writing and publication. Thank you for allowing yourself to be used by God and for being a friend to me and Darlene.

To all those who dedicated time and energy to read through early and later drafts of this book as it was being developed, thank you. The input I received was invaluable.

## Professional Supports

To all of those that contributed to my success, I want to thank you for believing in me. I chose not to identify you all by name, but many of you are described within its pages. If you helped me along the way, you know who you are. Without your support, I would not be where I am today. I pray that God blesses you richly for showing kindness to me.

# REFERENCES

*Scripture quotations marked (NIV) are taken from the Holy Bible, New International Version®, NIV®. Copyright © 1973, 1978, 1984, 2011 by Biblica, Inc.® Used by permission of Zondervan. All rights reserved worldwide. www.zondervan.com The "NIV" and "New International Version" are trademarks registered in the United States Patent and Trademark Office by Biblica, Inc.®*

Review of *RSTS Case Status Report*. 2006. Fresno Parole Office: CDCR.